SECOND EDITION

A DIFFERENT KIND OF
STRONG

{ Addiction & Adversity Leads To A
30-Day Fast & A Christ-Centered Life }

DANIEL L. TROTTER
with contributions from
Julianne Binkhurst Trotter & Daniel Craig Friend

To my loving wife, Julianne.

I appreciate all of your support and the many sacrifices that have made this book possible. Thank you for believing in me and loving me like no one else ever has. My sincerest gratitude to my family and many friends who have helped me along my journey. Most importantly, I would like to thank my Heavenly Father and his Son, Jesus Christ, my Savior, for saving me.

I SMOKED MY FIRST cigarette when I was seven years old. It was a clove cigarette, a little sweeter in smell and taste than tobacco, but that wasn't why I decided to try it. I did it because that's what everyone else at the canal that day was doing.

It was a dusty day in the scorching desert of Blythe, California, and two of my older brothers and I had gone swimming with a group of other kids. I think everyone there was older than me, and like most other kids who try drugs for the first time, I wanted to fit in—to be like the cool guys. My eight siblings and I had been raised as members of The Church of Jesus Christ of Latter-day Saints, but my brothers were already starting to follow a different path. Like many younger siblings, I wanted to follow them and our friends on what looked like an exciting, fun adventure.

So I inhaled the clove smoke. It smelled more inviting and less foul than tobacco, and even though I coughed and felt light-headed, the lingering taste was enough to remind me that I had done something that the cool kids did. I was one of them.

Besides, it was just one cigarette, right? How much harm could it do?

But it's never about just one cigarette. One leads to another, then another—or in my case, from one addiction to another. Next it was tobacco cigarettes. When my parents divorced, two of my brothers and I moved with my dad to San Clemente, and we made all the wrong friends. At age twelve, I was smoking marijuana and drinking alcohol in a pool hall, thanks to my brothers and our new connections. All this was just the beginning. By the time I was thirteen, I had done crack cocaine, mushrooms, even LSD. And I became addicted to pornography.

The most addictive and destructive drug I ever encountered was methamphetamine. I first tried it on my sixteenth birthday, in 1991. I had broken my right leg in a skateboarding accident and was wearing one of those medical boots to help it heal. My two oldest brothers took pity on me and decided to treat me to a night on the town. It started out as our standard bar experience—drinking, shooting pool, and enjoying ourselves—but on the way back out to the car, they mentioned they had some meth.

By that point, I'd tried almost everything else. I *wanted* to try it. A new high was the best kind of birthday present I could think of. As I sat alone in the back seat, my brother crushed the meth, chopped it up, and laid out a line of powder. I snorted it right up. It burned my nose worse than salt in an open wound, and then an awful, artificial taste of chemicals hit the back of my throat. I fought back simultaneous urges to gag and sneeze. That initial hit was fifty times worse than that first clove cigarette. But I was a tall, strong sixteen-year-old, and I wasn't going to let that show.

Then the high hit, and I didn't have to try.

It felt like an adrenaline rush that kept doubling and doubling until my mind was turbocharged. "Guys, I know exactly what I need to do!" I exclaimed, and then words rushed out of me faster than notes plucked during an electric guitar solo. It all seemed so clear. I was planning events and strategies, goals and objectives, and the drug not only showed my mind how to do it all but gave me the absolute assurance that I could and *would* accomplish all of it. I was on top of the world. I couldn't fail.

I barely noticed that my brothers were talking the same way I was; that we were talking over each other. The drug showed me what I wanted, not what was true. It didn't show me that this new addiction would lead me down a path that included drug busts, beatdowns, obsession, mental health issues, and an attempted suicide. And it certainly didn't show me that the only way I would be able to break the chains of my many addictions was to come back to the God and the religion I'd abandoned through an extreme fast—one like you read about in the Bible.

Addictions almost killed me, and breaking them almost killed me again. The only reason I am here to tell you this story is that I was saved by Jesus Christ.

My name is Daniel Trotter, and this is my story of redemption.

ON OCTOBER 14, 2011, I parked my blue Chrysler 300 at the entrance of Riverside State Park outside of Spokane, Washington. I went inside the small visitors' center and walked up to the park ranger behind the front desk.

"What can I do for you, sir?" she asked.

"I need a camping pass."

"How long do you plan to stay?"

I paused and chewed on that question for a minute. I had come up here, inspired by the biblical story of Jesus's fast in the wilderness recorded in Luke 4. After a prayer of desperation, I had opened my Bible not once, but twice to that same passage. I took it as a sign and surrendered to it. I didn't know exactly what I was looking for—only that I needed to come—and therefore I didn't know how long it would take for me to find what I needed. Thirty days? Forty? Fifty? I didn't know. I was out of work at the time, so I didn't have that responsibility, and my wife, Sally, had sensed that something was amiss in me and had encouraged me to make this pilgrimage. She wasn't expecting me back until I was done—whenever that was.

Christ had been in the wilderness for forty days. That

seemed like a good number to start with. "Forty days," I answered.

The ranger's mouth turned down in a frown. "Our longest pass is only thirty days," she said. "But you can buy another one once this one is up."

"Okay, a thirty-day pass it is, then." As I handed her my payment, I couldn't help but notice the little crease between her brows and the unspoken question behind it: What would I be doing in a state park for more than thirty days?

I doubt she would have guessed the real answer.

She handed me my pass. I thanked her, went back out to my car, and drove into the park. The clock in the dashboard read 11:00 a.m.

I hadn't eaten since nine the night before. And except for water, I wouldn't eat or drink anything else until God gave me the answers I sought. My fast had begun.

METH IS VERY DIFFERENT from most other drugs. First of all, it's not based on a natural source, like coca leaves for cocaine or poppy seeds for heroin (however processed those may become in the drug-making process). Meth is artificial from start to finish. Its chemical taste defies easy comparison. It's like reading those long, technical words for chemical substances with your tongue, and it leaves the same aftertaste.

The other difference is that, because it's so refined, meth's effects last much longer than most other drugs'. The initial high can keep you going for forty-eight hours with no sleep and no food. While cocaine's high may be more euphoric, it only lasts while you're using the drug. Hence, cocaine users generally need more of it to support their habit.

After barely graduating high school, I lived in the west side of Santa Cruz, California, with my brother Paul, who is my closest brother in age. Our drug of choice was cocaine.

We were living the beach party life in Santa Cruz. We met and partied with pro surfers, NFL players, a pro baseball player, and more beautiful girls than I can count. We were accepted everywhere, and feeling like we were a part of something for the first time in our lives was almost like a drug of its own. We needed to make sure that feeling didn't stop, so we drank hard and partied harder, and cocaine was a fixture at every event.

The best way to make sure you have a constant supply of a drug is to be the one selling it, and Paul and I worked our way into that niche. We gained a reputation as a reliable source. We were always holding some on us, and it was always profitable—we made money by *going* to parties.

Our best friends at the time were another pair of brothers, Oscar and Charlie. Charlie lived down the hall from our apartment; Oscar still lived at home with his parents. They were Mexican Americans, and they introduced us to a lot of our clientele. Oscar had a suave, charming smile in his clean-shaven face that contrasted heavily with his tattoos. Charlie, on the other hand, wore the Cheech Marin handlebar mustache and owned it for all it was worth. They were both amazingly fun to hang out with. Oscar was an aspiring DJ who wanted to be the life of every party, whether behind the turntable or in front of it. But Charlie was even better at it than Oscar. You couldn't have a conversation with the guy without laughing.

One night, at a party like any other, Charlie came back from getting another beer and plopped down on the couch next to Paul and me. He had the excited gleam in his eye that meant he'd scored something big.

"What is it?" I asked him.

Charlie just smiled and took a sip, pausing to wipe the foam off his mustache.

"Come on, man," Paul said. "You know you want to tell us."

Charlie smiled even bigger now. "I have a friend," he said, "who wants to make a deal."

"What kind of deal?" Paul asked.

"His name is Marc. He got out of prison recently, and he's got a friend from SoCal who wants some coke. A lot of coke. And I plan for us to get it for him."

"Yeah, so?" I said. Charlie was still smiling that mustached grin of his, meaning he hadn't told us the best part yet.

Paul made a guess at the good news. "How much does he want?"

"Only a low amount. A ki*lo*," he said, stretching out the syllable with the pun.

Paul barked a laugh. I whistled. A kilo wasn't a low amount at all. It's just over two pounds, and it was worth eighty grand. As the middlemen, we'd get a good amount of it for ourselves as a finder's fee. This was big-time.

"I need backup to make sure this all goes down right. You guys in?" Charlie asked.

Paul considered for a moment, looking into his beer. Then he looked at me. I shrugged, then nodded. Actually, I thought it sounded great.

"Yeah," Paul said to Charlie, "we're in."

Crime isn't actually any less work than a regular job; the logistics are as complicated as any other business. A deal like the one Charlie had found doesn't just happen. First we had to contact our supplier, then run messages between him and the buyer while they negotiated price (which took several meetings), then finally schedule the time and place of the actual trade. And of course, in the meantime, we were drinking and partying like always, only this time we'd wave hundred-dollar bills in the air and argue loud and jokingly about whose turn it was to pay. We were acting like we'd already made the deal, but of course we hadn't. All we were doing was drawing attention to ourselves.

On the day of the big exchange, after working all day at my job in construction, I went to Charlie's apartment. Charlie greeted me at the door, more excited and anxious than I'd ever seen him—I could tell because for once, he wasn't cracking a joke. "We're about to do this!" was all he said. Inside the apartment, my brother Paul was sitting on the couch across from our supplier. The buyer, Marc, wasn't there yet. Charlie closed the door behind me, and I realized he was holding a pistol in one hand.

I glanced toward Paul and our supplier. They had guns too.

My blood ran cold. I'd been around guns from time to time, but they'd never been my thing. Now I was in a room with three people packing. It seemed ominous.

"What's going on?" I asked.

"We have to be ready," my brother said. "You never know when a deal like this could go sideways. We're about to sell a kilo here." He locked eyes with me, and his expression was the one he wore whenever he was doing something to protect his younger brother, me. I'd seen it a few times in Santa Cruz, and I knew to trust it.

"Sure," I said. "I get it."

Paul nodded at Charlie, who turned around and offered me another pistol.

"In case anything happens," he said. "Take this. And be prepared."

Slowly, I reached for the butt of the weapon. What kind of gun was this? I had no idea, and I still don't. My hand closed around the metal grip, and I realized I was still filthy from work. "I need to take a shower," I said. "Do I have time?"

The three exchanged glances, and the supplier nodded. I hid the gun in my pants and then went back down the hall to my own apartment. I jumped in the shower and scrubbed the dirt of the construction site from my skin. Just as I was finishing, someone knocked on my apartment door. I threw a towel around my waist and answered it. It was my neighbor from across the hall. Her eyes were wide as she asked, "Do you know what's going on at Charlie's? There are cops every-where!"

My stomach dropped like a lead weight. I excused myself and got dressed as quickly as I could, put the gun out of sight, and went down the hall to see what was going on. An alphabet soup of jackets confronted my eyes: Santa Cruz PD, FBI, FDA, ATF. Agents swarmed the apartment building. Charlie's door had been broken down. I tried to get a glimpse of Charlie and Paul, but an agent stopped me and told me to stay back. As I obeyed, I wondered if they knew who I was—not that I was about to tell them, of course. So I sat in front of the building and waited. Eventually, the parade of handcuffs started— Charlie, his head drooping more than his mustache ever did, all the comedy gone from his eyes; our supplier, looking defiant and shooting glares at everyone; and finally, my brother Paul, who looked bewildered, as though he couldn't believe what was happening to him. We locked eyes again for a second, and a sad smile tugged at one corner of his mouth. I like to think it meant, "At least you're not in handcuffs too."

And that was it. Charlie's "friend" Marc and his friend, the buyer, were nowhere to be seen. What the heck?

I called Oscar, Charlie's brother. When he picked up, I said, "Dude, the cops just raided your brother's place. Charlie and Paul have been arrested."

Oscar swore, then asked, "Do you know what they found?"

"We were about to sell the kilo; there's no way they didn't find it. And everyone had a gun too."

Oscar swore again. "Guns in that type of deal mean extra trouble." He paused for a second, then added a few choice expletives as he guessed that Marc, Charlie's friend, had sold us out. "They might come after you next," he added. "Do you have anything in your place?"

"A pound of pot in my closet, some coke—and the gun Charlie gave me right before it happened." Now it was my turn to swear.

"You gotta get rid of 'em, man. You could be next."

"Can you take them to your place?" I asked.

"That's risky, man. They might be watching you."

"We'll wait till it calms down."

Waiting for all the cops to leave was nerve-racking. Each glance my direction seemed like an unspoken accusation. But they never asked me any questions or came to my apartment. Eventually, they all left, and I took my contraband to Oscar without incident. As I handed him the marijuana, coke, and gun, he asked me, "Hey, man, so how in the world did you not get busted too? You were supposed to be there, right?"

"I was, but . . ." It sounded so stupid to say it out loud. "I went to take a shower." I shrugged. "Dumb luck, I guess."

As I SET UP MY campsite in Riverside State Park, for some reason, that old memory of escaping the drug bust in Santa Cruz flashed through my mind. It turned out our buyer really had rolled over on us, and Charlie and Paul each got three years in prison after making a plea deal. My name had been on every investigation document, but since I hadn't been at the scene of the crime, the police hadn't been able to charge me with anything. If it hadn't been for that shower, I would've been right there with them. And I don't think I would have done well in prison.

I looked up at the sky through the evergreen trees and prayed, thanking God that I had not been arrested that day. And the thought came back that my desire to shower, and ironically, to feel clean, had been a mercy from God. A simple yet significant and tender mercy—one that I did not in any way deserve on my own merits.

Sometimes God saves you from things simply because he loves you. Sometimes we don't let him do that.

Once my camp was set up, I took a hike to explore the surrounding area. My stomach growled, but I ignored it.

I found my way up to a bench overlooking the Spokane

River. It was a beautiful day. The river reflected the few clouds of billowy white that traversed the sky. Pine trees stood, stately and elegant, like an army about to march down the rise and cross the river. Birds flew overhead. This was serenity.

And yet I couldn't help reflecting on how different this moment was from so many years of my past. I didn't stop dealing or using after Paul and Charlie's arrest. Being saved from arrest hadn't changed me in any significant way. And even this vista, as impressive and inspiring as it was, would have just as momentary an impact on my life . . . unless . . .

Unless I stopped being a pawn that things happened *to* and started being the one who made things happen. Dumb luck, divine mercy, call it what you will—that wasn't going to be enough without action from me. I'd learned as much in subsequent years as a personal trainer. I had to be self-motivated, to keep working hard under my own discipline, or else nothing would change.

And that's what I'd come out here to do. I wouldn't be the 98 percent of people who didn't keep their New Year's resolutions or meet their gym goals. I would overcome because I would keep working and fighting no matter how hard it got. Out here, I would overcome my physical wants—a fast in the true sense of the word.

I picked up a stick on the ground—a good stick, straight, with a little bit of weight to it—and used it to carve seven letters in the dirt at my feet:

VICTORY

As I finished the final arm of the *Y,* sounds drew my gaze heavenward. I looked up. A flock of geese soared above me, honking as they flew south in a perfect *V* formation. *V* for victory.

I knew it was a sign. Victory would be mine. In that moment, I knew that God and I were going to accomplish what we had set out to do. I needed help, and this was God's way of telling me that I was not alone and I was protected. God was with me.

With God, nothing is impossible. Even transforming a life like mine.

*And the Spirit brought him to Jerusa-
lem, and set him on a pinnacle of the temple.
And the devil came unto him, and said, If
thou be the Son of God, cast thyself down
from hence. (JST Luke 4:9)*

FULL OF THE FEELING OF victory after the sign of the geese, I
continued exploring Riverside State Park. I hiked up a nearby
rise and eventually found myself at the top of a steep cliff
overlooking the river. The view was breathtaking. Rapids
churned with white foam around giant boulders, placed there
millennia ago by divine hands working through massive
glaciers. Elegant evergreens stood in stately regiments along
the gentler slope of the far bank, pointing straight up to
heaven.

I walked up to the cliff's edge and glanced down. The
riverbank seemed almost exactly below me—dozens of yards
down. What if I fell? I half expected to feel vertigo, but I didn't.
Instead, a thought entered my mind, as quiet as a whisper:
What if you jumped?

I should have pushed the impression away, but instead, I
thought about it. I imagined my body flying through the air,
weightless for an extended instant, then hurtling downward

as a scream tore its way from my throat. I wouldn't land in the water—no, that was too far away, no matter how it looked from up here—but rather on one of those giant boulders, probably headfirst, with a sickening *smack*.

I knew what that would feel like, in the instant before it would all go black. I knew because I'd felt something very much like it before.

MY BROTHER'S PRISON TIME did nothing to reform him. After he got out, we were back to our old habits in Santa Cruz in no time. I eventually moved in with Oscar, Charlie's younger brother. Since our brothers' drug bust, we'd grown closer, becoming like brothers ourselves. We did everything together, from drinking to drugs to picking up girls.

The party that night started out like any other: booze and drugs at a warehouse down the street, hosted by some surfer, the music playing so loud you almost had to yell to make conversation. The difference was that about halfway through the night, as Charlie, Oscar, and I walked outside to get some fresh air, we saw three new people out in the street, trying to get into the party. Mexican American, lean muscled, and full mustached, wearing hoodies, they sauntered around like they owned the place. Even through my cocaine-and-alcohol-addled vision, I recognized them as belonging to one of the local gangs. In fact, they lived down the street from me. I didn't know who'd invited them to this party—if anyone—but I knew I didn't like them being there.

And I wasn't the only one. At the moment we arrived, they were arguing with a couple of girls we knew—friends of ours, though nothing serious had ever happened between them and any of us. But they were telling these guys exactly what I wanted to:

"We don't want you here, capisce? You guys ruin every party you come to. You need to go home. Right now."

But that didn't stop these gangsters. On the contrary—a girl protesting just meant she secretly wanted more and was playing hard to get.

"What?" the closest gangster said. "You don't want me here? You want me to go home? That must mean you want to go home with me, 'cause I know you want some-a this." He unzipped his hoodie halfway, exposing tattooed pecs. You could barely see him flex beneath all the ink.

My friend wrinkled her nose and told him exactly how attractive she found *that* offer.

The gangster said something about how pretty she was as his hand found its way onto her hip. She slapped it away, and he and his buddies laughed.

I decided it was time to intervene. I stepped closer, swayed, and steadied myself. "Hey," I said.

They ignored me, so I said it again, louder. "Hey. What are you, deaf? Didn't you hear her the first two times she said 'get lost'?"

The ringleader drew himself up to his full height of five feet, zero inches as he stood and sized me up through narrowed eyes.

"What you got to say about it?" he asked, spitting out a Spanish expletive to tell me exactly what he thought of my opinion.

"Leave her alone. And her friend too," I added.

"Or what?" he asked, all attitude. "What you gonna do about it?"

I suddenly realized that his two buddies were flanking him, their hands curled into fists. I might have had a good foot and a half on them, but three on one is losing odds for anyone who's not a black belt in something.

I felt a hand on my shoulder. I glanced over to see Oscar and Charlie by my side. Maybe the odds weren't so bad after all. Then Oscar said, "Come on, Danny. Let's go."

"But—"

The gangsters laughed as Oscar started pulling me away and I stumbled after him. Once we were around the warehouse's corner, by Oscar's truck, I shook Oscar off me. "Why'd you do that, man? I could've taken them!"

Oscar shook his head. "They're gangsters, man. One of 'em's gotta have a knife or something." I looked into his eyes. He was almost as drunk and high as I was. Almost. "We gotta have something better."

He was right; I could tell that. But I was drawing a total blank about where to get "something better."

Then Oscar's eyes lit up. "Baseball bats," he said, smiling to himself. "I got some back at my place."

I nodded. "What are we waiting for?"

Oscar's house was close by, and it took us only a few minutes to drive there in his truck, retrieve a trio of Louisville sluggers, and come back armed. Not long enough for the gangsters to have made any serious moves on our friends. I hoped.

It was a cool night, but I was sweating a little in anticipation as we pulled up to the party warehouse. I scratched at my scalp beneath my beanie, and some part of my brain remembered that I really ought to shave my head again.

We found both our friends and the gangsters right where we'd left them, on the street outside the party. I called out to the ringleader with an English expletive on par with the one he'd given me.

He turned around, and his annoyance morphed into surprise when he saw our bats.

Then he laughed and pulled a GLOCK from his waistband.

His buddies produced similar weapons, and before I knew what was happening, they took away my bat and then Oscar's and Charlie's. The ringleader pressed the barrel of his gun into my spine. "So what's your big mouth got to say now, eh, white boy? All outta words? I oughta kill you right now for what you said to me. And if you say anything else, I swear to

God, I will put a bullet through you right now, you hear what I'm saying?"

The street had gone silent except for music still blaring from the building. I could feel my pulse pounding in my ears, and over and over in my head came two phrases as if on repeat: *That's not how I expected this to go*, and, *Never bring a bat to a gunfight, idiot.*

I glanced over at Oscar and Charlie. Since they were locals, born and raised on the west side of Santa Cruz, they didn't have any guns pointed at them. But they certainly couldn't make a move without me getting shot. The girls were on the sidewalk, clinging to each other. A crowd of partygoers was forming behind them, watching the confrontation. I recognized several faces, but they couldn't help me any more than Charlie or Oscar could. The final gang member spun Oscar's bat idly in one hand, holding mine with the other.

And now that he had a "captive" audience, their leader would not shut up. "You even *move* now, I kill you. You understand? You gotta be some kind of stupid, coming back here to mess with us. With *me*. You nothin', you got that? I kill you right now, no one cares. No one cry for you but your mama. So don't you say nothing, or you die tonight."

He kept asking questions like he expected some kind of answer but in the same breath would threaten to kill me if I spoke. "You got no right to tell any of us who we can and can't talk to, *comprende*? We don't listen to you. You white trash. You nothin' to us. You *dead*, you say anything!"

I was high, I was drunk, and I was tired of this guy's threats, so I said, "Fine. Go ahead. Pull the trigger."

Someone gasped, and the gangster stumbled in his posturing monologue. *Weren't expecting to hear that, were you?* I thought with grim satisfaction.

Then, from the sidelines, one of my friends in the crowd yelled, "Danny, look out!" I turned my head toward the sound of his voice, and for a split second, woodgrain filled my vision.

The bat met my head with a dull slap. I stumbled backward, dazed but still conscious. I raised my hand to my beanie. My fingers came away wet and red.

The gang leader laughed. "That's what you get!" he crowed. "And don't you forget it!"

One of his buddies, seeing the blood on the bat, said, "Come on, man, let's go." They tossed our bats aside and left.

They hadn't been gone five minutes when a half dozen Santa Cruz police officers showed up to bust the party.

Half an hour later, one of the cops was trying to convince me to get inside an ambulance.

"No," I said. "I don't want to."

"You have blood all over your sweater, and your beanie is practically soaked. You need to go to the hospital, sir."

"I—I'll be fine," I lied.

"The only way you can refuse a ride is if you correctly answer a series of questions to prove you don't have a concussion," he said.

"Okay," I said. I was uninsured; I couldn't afford an ambulance ride. So I answered his list of questions, and somehow, I got them all right.

He sighed as I finished the last one. "Okay, I can't legally force you to get into this vehicle, but you really need to have that looked at, you hear?"

I nodded, and an hour or so later, I made my own way to an emergency room and got myself stitched up. By that time, the lump on my head was literally the size of a baseball. The doctor who did the stitching kept on shaking her head. "You're lucky to be alive, Mr. Trotter." She looked at my blood-soaked beanie in amazement, and I could tell she was wondering how that hat alone had cushioned my head so well. I was wondering the same thing. "You are *so* lucky to be alive."

———— ◆ ————

I WAS LUCKY TO be alive—not only after that but after several other experiences. I stepped back from the cliff's edge. I knew what that smack at the bottom would feel like—like the bat hitting my head, except over every inch of my body at once. No. No, jumping now would be the height of ingratitude. Especially after everything God had done for me—including giving me his promise of victory not an hour earlier.

I couldn't stop now. I would see my fast through to its end.

I started walking back toward my campsite, and as I wended my way through stands of pine trees, I reflected on the unlikely sequel of that bat incident, which happened nearly a decade after the assault.

"REMEMBER THE GUY WHO pulled a gun on you at that party back in '98?" my brother Paul asked me.

"The punk who used to live a block down the street?"

"Yeah, that guy."

"How could I forget?" I replied. "He had his friend give me this with my own bat." I pointed at a scar on my forehead.

"Yeah, well, he and his buddies have been following me around lately. Seems they think I had something to do with that."

I sputtered with incomprehension. "You were barely out of prison then—and you weren't even at that party!"

Paul nodded in exasperation. "I know. I tried to tell him that, but he just won't get the message."

"That sounds familiar." I didn't say anything else, but the wheels in my head were turning. The rest of my trip to California had been an absolute disaster. But if I could make things a little better for Paul, then it might not be a total loss. *It's not like I've got anything to lose*, I thought to myself. As soon as Paul left the room, I went outside, jumped in my car, and drove to a house I remembered from almost ten years before. I parked and knocked on the door. The very same gangster who hit me with the bat answered. I pointed at the scar on my forehead and asked, "Do you remember me?"

He looked me up and down, obviously surprised and nervous, then answered, "Yeah, I remember you."

"I hear you've been following my brother around town. Paul Trotter."

"I ain't got nothin' to do with him."

"That's not what I hear," I countered, "but you'd better have nothing to do with him, because he has nothing to do with us. That thing that happened years ago, with the bat? That was between you and me. No one else. Paul wasn't even at that party. But if you've still got a problem with *me* for what happened there, then we can settle this right now, in your front yard, man-to-man."

He sized me up again, then leaned against his doorjamb. "Nah," he said. "I don't think we needa do that."

I stopped in my tracks. I had been ready to knock this guy out, get hit by another bat, or even get shot for real this time. But instead of being all confrontational like he had been at the party years ago, now this man seemed . . . uneasy. Nervous. Scared. Almost like he wasn't the same gangster he had been.

And I realized that I felt that way too.

"Look," I said, "I'm not the same person that I was back

then. I don't party anymore. I don't even live in this *state* anymore, and I don't plan to ever again. Once I leave here today, you never have to see me or worry about me ever again. All I want is for you to leave my brother alone—'cause he has nothing to do with any of this—and maybe see if there's some way for things to be okay between you and me. 'Cause I don't need this crap hanging over me for the rest of my life. Do you?"

He thought about it a minute, then shook his head. Silence stretched between us for a moment.

Finally, I said, "So . . . we cool, then?"

He stood up straight and looked me in the eye. "Yeah, we're cool. I'm over it."

"Okay," I said. And then I offered him my hand.

He seemed surprised, but then he took my hand and shook it. And in his eyes, the nervousness I'd seen when he'd answered the door melted away, replaced by something you could even call respect.

I nodded, walked back to my car, and drove away. I called Paul and told him I'd taken care of his stalker problem. He was impressed—"You just come to town and take care of business, Danny!" I've never seen that gangster since, but I think we learned something from each other that day. There's a peace that comes from forgiving others, especially people who have hurt you badly in the past. Letting go of that pain allows us to move on, to progress to the next phase of life and grow into the people we need to become. I'd carried the baggage of that grudge with me for many years. I felt thirty pounds lighter after dropping it off at that house in Santa Cruz.

PERHAPS AS A RESULT of seeing the cliff that first afternoon in Riverside State Park, there was a cliff in my dream not long after. The beautiful landscape I'd admired before was now consumed in orange flame. Even in my dreaming state, I recognized those evil embers: they represented the depths of hell. In their dancing flames, I could see each addiction I'd yielded to; in the curl of the smoke, every act of violence I'd committed.

I turned and locked eyes with a fantastically gigantic snake positioned between me and freedom. I took a pace back in surprise, and my heel brushed the edge of the cliff. I had nowhere to go. The serpent had me trapped.

My hands curled into fists.

The serpent struck, and I dodged to the side. It coiled up, then lunged for me again, mouth agape, but this time I was ready. I swung my left fist in an uppercut that deflected the serpent's head. It tried to come at me from behind, and I barely ducked in time. I stumbled, and I realized my foot was caught in one of the serpent's giant coils. I fought to free it, but the snake squeezed tighter. Its mouth opened in a silent, mocking laugh. Its body circled closer, and its breath was the same hot brimstone scent as the valley below. Its forked tongue flicked out, tickling at my ear.

I slapped the tongue away and threw a right cross at the serpent's eye. It dodged backward, surprised, and its hold around my leg loosened. I rolled to my right, trying to put some distance between myself and the cliff's edge, but the snake's tail was waiting for me. It smacked me in the chest and flung me back toward the cliff.

I skidded to a stop, my head hanging over the edge of the chasm. Somehow I knew that I wouldn't die if I went over it, but rather, I would be in this beast's power for as long as it wanted me. And I saw in the cold blackness of its eyes that it would never let me go.

I had to win this fight.

I rolled up to a crouch, then settled into a fighting stance. The enormous serpent let me, seemingly amused. Its tongue flicked out again. Then it lowered its head and slithered slowly closer.

When the next strike came, I barely saw it in time to block. The next one came just as quickly, and from the other side. I stumbled toward the edge of the cliff and fought to keep my balance. Waiting for it to strike wasn't working, so I charged at it instead.

I connected with a left to its nose, then a right below its eye. It reared its head back and hissed in fury. I delivered a solid kick to its underbelly.

The thing struck back ferociously. I blocked and dodged and counterstruck with a fierce determination not to be owned by this abomination, all the while circling just a tiny bit—too tiny for the beast to notice.

Finally, after what seemed like a lifetime, our positions were correct. The serpent hissed again and dove right at me, jaws gaping.

I sidestepped and delivered the finest roundhouse kick I had ever executed to the side of the creature's head. The force of my blow sent the serpent over the side of its own cliff.

I awoke and tried to steady my breathing. My ragged gasps settled down into a normal, waking rhythm, and I grappled with what I had just dreamed.

I had been taught that Satan was real. Not just a personification of abstract evil but an actual being with a personal vendetta against God's children. Now I felt that malice personally. I knew my addictions had kept me trapped at various points in my life. And my struggle to break free of all that they entailed—the fast that I was now on the fifth day of—would be just as hard and brutal and real a struggle as my battle with the serpent had seemed in my dream. It might not appear as well defined in the waking world, but the consequences would be as momentous as falling from a cliffside into an inferno.

I relieved some of my body's tension by taking a dip in a nearby stream. The water was shockingly cold but refreshing. I dried myself off and returned to my campsite, sitting by the ashes of my fire from the night before. I'd been sleeping longer than usual the last few days—a side effect of my fast, I reckoned—and the embers from last night had grown cold. I was debating starting another blaze when movement at the edge of the campsite caught my eye.

It was a family of deer—a doe, a buck, and a fawn. I stilled my muscles and slowed my breathing. Suddenly it was the most important thing in the world not to scare them.

They picked their way through my campsite, heading toward the hill on the opposite side. They were beautiful, their coats a perfect brown, the buck's antlers small but stately. Their eyes were mesmerizing. I stared at them, and they stared back at me. I think they sensed my calm. Despite the dream I'd had, I'd found with these animals a moment of perfect tranquility. They seemed to know I posed no threat.

"I'm not going to hurt you," I said softly.

The look in their eyes showed me that they'd already recognized that.

"You're beautiful, by the way. I've never seen a deer this close before."

They stopped for a minute in the center of my campground. The buck turned his head. The whole family looked at me, almost as if waiting for something.

In that moment I felt a tender serenity, a oneness with nature that I'd never felt before. And I realized that I had never been as at peace with myself as I was in that moment. I was so at peace that even these wild animals could sense my tranquility and approach me this closely.

"Thank you for coming by to see me," I said. "I think I needed this today." Some polite part of my mind reminded me that it was rude to detain others who had things to do. "Thank you," I repeated. "Goodbye."

And then, as though I'd given them permission, they finished crossing my campground and began climbing the hill, fawn first and adults following, in much the same way that shepherds herd their flocks.

I leaned back, closed my eyes, and sighed a prayer of thanksgiving heavenward.

BY DAY EIGHT, MAKING a fire each night became a taxing chore. My body had switched from using up reserves to burning muscle, and though I had a good amount of that at the start of my fast, it wasn't an infinite source. But it was one I was willing to sacrifice.

The chore of fire building began taking up the better part of my afternoons. I had to drive to take trips away from camp by now. My stomach had ceased growling days ago; now it simply ached beneath my lungs, a dull and constant throb I learned to ignore. I'd brought firewood with me, but finding the kindling I needed for my campfires kept me occupied. It was about all my body had the strength to do.

I chuckled at that thought. I was a licensed personal trainer; I'd met my wife, Sally, at the gym. And here I was, barely able to pick up sticks off the ground. I'd never felt this weak before.

Once, years earlier, I'd been strong enough to knock a man out with a single punch.

IN LATE 2001, I was living at my father and stepmother's house in San Clemente, California, with my older brother Clint. He was the second oldest of my parents' sons, and I was, of course, still the youngest. Despite the age difference, we'd lived pretty similar lives. Clint was one of my brothers who had been present when I tried meth for the first time at sixteen.

At this point, though, we were simply drinking at a bar, trying to dull away the anger we felt at the world for a lifetime of frustrated ambitions. I'd always wanted to make music, but no real opportunities had ever come my way. My meth use didn't help at all, but I couldn't see that at the time. Back then, all I could see was how meth let me play and create for hours on end. But the frustration at that and a million other little failures continued to grow and fester, building up like a soda bottle being shaken continuously—all it would take was one little twist to make me explode.

That night, some guys came in and sat down near us. They were the standard dingy lowlifes you'd expect to find in a dingy bar—guys who'd pretend they were something dangerous to try and hide the fact that they were never going to choose to rise above the gutter they swam in.

These four guys had barely sipped their drinks before one

of them started gesturing at Clint and me with his stubbly chin.

"How 'bout them? Double jump." His companions laughed.

I swung around on my barstool and faced them. "You got something to say to us? Come on, let me hear it."

The guys mumbled and looked into their drinks. "Nothing, man."

I shot a cockeyed grin at Clint. "Well, that's good, 'cause I thought I heard those idiots were planning to jump us."

Clint and I shared a rowdy laugh and turned back to our booze. Pretty soon, three of the four hooligans left—but the last one came right up to us, an angry glare on his face.

"You guys are lucky," he said, pausing for a dramatic effect that fell spectacularly flat, "tonight, that is."

I raised an eyebrow. "Oh? And why is that?"

"We was gonna jump you two fools tonight. But we got better things to do. So you're lucky."

Clint looked like he was going to burst into giggles. I looked at the young hoodlum with mock sincerity. "Why would you want to do that?" I asked. "You'd just get knocked out."

Clint thought that was pretty funny. Our would-be jumper was less amused. His face screwed up in rage, and he stormed out, yelling profanities over his shoulder at me as he left.

Alcohol can make you shift from jovial to violent in an instant—especially when it's sloshing around a meth user's brain. The insults pushed me over a line that the threat of jumping never even came close to. I slammed my glass down on the bar and followed the guy outside.

"What did you call me? What did you say?" I yelled after him.

He turned around, a cocky sneer set on a face ready to repeat every insult he'd lobbed at me. He didn't have to utter a single syllable; it was, to my drunken mind, like he'd already said it all and more.

The anger I'd been trying to drink away thundered up inside me like an erupting volcano. Alcohol doesn't actually make problems go away; the best it can do is hide them for an evening, at most. But that lie never lasts.

A buddy of mine had once taught me how to knock someone out in a single punch, and that's exactly what I did. All the anger I'd built up over the years found its way into a mighty right cross aimed right for his chin. The punch connected, his chin obligingly split open, and he fell forward toward me as he lost consciousness. I brushed him to the side like he was a single strand of beaded curtain. As his body hurtled toward the asphalt below, I said with nonchalance, "I told you that you were going to get knocked out."

"What's going on here?" an angry voice called from

behind me. I saw the bartender walking out of the bar. My brother tagged behind her, half apologetically. "We don't *do* that here!" the bartender spluttered at me, her face growing red.

"Tonight, you do," I said, looking her in the eye.

Then the bartender backed off.

My brother came up beside me and said soothingly, "We should go. The cops could be here any minute."

I nodded, and we left.

As soon as the adrenaline wore off, I started feeling guilty. I've read since then that you can't knock someone unconscious without causing a certain amount of brain damage. I'm not sure if I knew that fact at the time, but I wished I hadn't done it. No insult is worth that kind of serious hurt. Clint and I were never really in danger, and my violent response was totally unwarranted.

Nights like that eventually moved my dad to kick us out of his home. Once again, I was homeless, couch surfing between friends' apartments, a friend's car, and the occasional hotel, always looking for the next high, the next party, the next girl.

Meth ruled my life at this time. Like every addict, I kept chasing the elusive feeling of that first amazing high, when my brain was first exposed to a chemical it had no tolerance for. But that feeling can never, ever come twice. Human physiology prohibits it.

And meth has very different aftereffects than other drugs. All drugs, by definition, change the way the mind stores and/or processes information, but meth's effects not only last a long time after the high has faded but are cumulative. The brain keeps morphing as the addict goes through the cycle. Methamphetamines made me paranoid. Little coincidences took on exaggerated meanings. I became convinced that most of my friends were out to get me, though I couldn't articulate why. Sounds and sights and other stimuli over energized my neurons, and I interpreted in them so much more than there could possibly be. It didn't matter that it made no sense; that was only further evidence that the people out to get me were everywhere.

I was in no way sober, but even in that condition, amid constant bad decisions, I did decide to do one thing right. I had an outstanding warrant for my arrest back in Santa Cruz—a DUI for drinking and driving. The state had already suspended, then revoked my driver's license for failing to take care of it. For whatever reason, even though I knew it would force me to get sober (or perhaps, a little, because of that fact), I decided to turn myself in and take care of it.

I somehow scraped together enough money for a plane ticket, and in late 2002, I flew back up to Northern California. Before I left, though, I bought two grams of meth and smuggled it on to the plane with me. Risks like that don't matter to a drug addict. I knew I was going to be sober soon, so I was going to party it up before I went to jail.

My buddy Alan picked me up from the airport. He was about five foot ten, bald, goateed, a little broader in the shoulders than me, and a natural at sports. He was also the most original person I've ever met. Rocky Balboa was his personal hero, yet Alan would party harder and longer than anyone else I knew. "Ready for your last week of freedom, Danny?" he asked me with a slap on the back.

"You know it! Look what I brought." I flashed him the meth.

Colorful language punctuated his excitement. "Drinks now or later?" he asked.

"Both," I said. "Definitely both."

By the time we got to "drinks later" at Alan's place, a group of friends had come over to party with us. Among them was a blonde-haired, brown-eyed girl that Alan took great pleasure in introducing to me.

"Danny, this is Mary."

She held out a dainty hand, and I shook it. "I think we've met before," I said, but through the buzz of alcohol, I couldn't remember where or when.

She flashed an absolutely gorgeous smile with perfect, straight white teeth. When she spoke, her voice was soft and sweet. "Yes, of course!" she replied, recalling the exact event as she wrapped her free arm around my friend's waist. Her head barely came up to the middle of his chest. But then, I've always been attracted to shorter girls with petite builds like Mary's.

"You look good together," I said, raising my beer in a salute. "How long has this been going on?"

"Oh, a few months now," Alan said, giving Mary's spaghetti-strapped shoulder a caress.

"Well, congratulations. And good job, man," I added with a thumbs-up.

Mary laughed like an angel, and we returned to the party.

But after a week, my meth ran out, and it was time to turn myself in. At the Santa Cruz courthouse, I pleaded guilty, and the judge read off my fine. I stood in a setting that was as grim and sober and sterile as the previous week had been rowdy and carefree and colorful, and said, "Your honor, I have no money to pay off this fine."

"In that case, Mr. Trotter, I can sentence you to forty-five days in jail. It's that or the fine—your choice."

"All I have to offer is my time. I'll take the forty-five days."

He nodded. "Very well. Daniel L. Trotter, I hereby sentence you to forty-five days' imprisonment. You will report to the Santa Cruz County Jail tomorrow morning by 10 a.m. If you do not report . . ." He continued reading off all the legalese he had to, then gaveled the court into adjournment.

I walked out of that room feeling . . . different than I'd expected. I wasn't looking forward to a month and a half in jail, but I wasn't dreading it either. Part of me wanted nothing more than just to get the whole thing over with. But another part of me felt freer walking out of that courthouse than I had walking in. I realized, in hindsight, that I was feeling the freedom that comes from taking responsibility for one's actions and making restitution for one's mistakes. I know now that without taking this vital step, no one can ever change their lives for good. This part of coming back to the light takes different forms for different people. For myself, I was nowhere close to done by taking this single step. This one action in no way guaranteed the absolution I eventually found. But it was an important and necessary first step in my journey, as it is in every path to repentance. Walking into the California sun that day, I felt honest about my actions for the first time in a long while. I may have escaped arrest for a time, but that dishonesty weighed down my spirit as surely as any earthly shackles. And I hadn't even felt the load until they were removed.

I spent only a couple of days at the county jail before I was transferred to "the Farm," also known as "Camp Snoopy" to many of the inmates. It was less of a jail and more of a camp out in the middle of nowhere—it didn't even have a fence. Of course, if you did walk off the grounds, you'd pay the price by doing even more time when you were caught.

Time spent doing work release kept my mind off where I was. Some inmates tried to look tough by forming racial cliques within the camp, like they were at a regular prison. I just laughed at them and walked away (which would not have gone over as well in prison). I had a couple of Mexican friends doing time at Camp Snoopy with me, and I wasn't going to turn my back on them just because a couple of wannabes thought they were in San Quentin.

After twenty-eight days, I was released for good behavior—and I was on my way to sobriety. In fact, I made a resolution to be done with partying.

Alan picked me up and took me to his house. "You've been gone for almost a month, Danny—I bet you're thirsty. Want a beer?"

"No thanks," I said, sticking to my resolution.

Alan shrugged and helped himself to a bottle from the fridge. "Suit yourself. Have a seat."

I made myself comfortable in his recliner while he flopped down on the couch. Mary snuggled up next to him.

"So how was the Farm?" Alan asked.

"Not that bad, surprisingly. I mean, it was cold, and the beds sucked, but the food was better than you'd expect."

"No kidding."

"Were there gangs?" Mary asked. She sounded so innocent. I knew better though—I mean, she'd seen everything Alan and I had done during my week of partying—but it was hard to shake that impression of angelic, childlike innocence.

I chuckled. "A couple of morons tried to start one—you know, 'Don't buy cigarettes from people who are not of your race; stick to your own kind or else!'—but almost no one took 'em seriously. I didn't, anyway."

"Wow," Mary said, sounding impressed.

"So what are you going to do now?" Alan asked.

"I dunno," I said. "I think I might start running—you know, take care of myself better."

"Good for you!" Mary's smile was radiant.

"Drugs and party days behind you?" Alan asked.

"Yeah. I think I might want to try out being your guys' designated driver or something."

"Oh, that'd be great!" they both said.

"But wait," Alan said, "I thought you didn't have a license."

"I'll figure something out. And maybe I'll get back in touch with some old friends while I'm here."

"Well," Alan said, "my couch is your couch for as long as you need."

———— ◆ ————

I POKED MY CAMPFIRE with a stick, and sparks flew up, distracting me from my memory. The night was cold, and my body ached from days without food. The fire was getting low. I stirred the embers again, thinking about turning in for the night, when I heard what sounded like a dog howling in the distance. *What's a stray dog doing in a state park?* my tired brain wondered.

Then a second howl joined the first. Then a third, then a fourth.

Wolves, I thought. I was sure of it.

And the howls were getting closer.

You should leave. The thought entered my head without warning.

"No," I said aloud. I'd promised God I wouldn't leave until I got my answers.

The canines called again, louder. Anxiety grew in my chest. What if they found me here, weakened from my fast?

You won't be able to defend yourself, a voice said inside my head. *They'll tear you into pieces.*

The howls reverberated through the night. They picked up speed, each one answered faster than before.

You can't fight them. Give up and leave while you still can.

Terror gripped my heart. My breath came out in ragged gasps.

Are you really going to let yourself be killed for a foolish fast that won't work?

Why was my mind trying to make me veer from the path I'd chosen? It made no sense. And then I realized: my mind was not the source of these thoughts.

As I sat at the campfire, I summoned all my courage and resolve and called out my adversary. "Satan, show yourself!" I yelled. "I know you're there. I know it's you trying to make me run. Well, it won't work! I won't budge. You can't stop me—nothing can. I will do this even if I die trying, so do your worst! Show yourself, and let's take care of this once and for all."

The night went silent. The darkness left my mind.

Satan never showed himself to me. That's when I learned that for all his craftiness and cunning, Lucifer's a coward. He can't stand up to a determined human soul. But he is real nonetheless and will do everything within his power to make us doubt ourselves and abandon God.

I finally went to sleep, and this time, my dreams reflected the real-life battle I'd just fought. The serpent from my prior dream was back, but this time he was smaller—a normal-size snake—and instead of a constrictor, he was a viper, fangs bared and coiled up to strike.

"This one will not be defeated until its head is severed clean," a voice informed me. "Look down."

I looked down at my hands, and into them was placed a sword. My fingers wrapped around the hilt. I'd never used a sword in real life, but in this dream, I knew how to use it. I tested it for weight and balance and realized I was a master of this weapon. I stepped into the ring and raised my sword to my opponent.

The snake struck blindingly fast. I barely stepped aside in time. I whipped the tip of my blade after it and missed. The viper was already launching itself at me again. I threw myself to the side and rolled away, keeping tight hold of my sword. I picked myself up from the dust. My enemy was already coiled up and hissing.

The strike came in like lightning. I blocked and leaped backward. The viper nipped my clothes, but I was unscathed. I swung and thrust my blade, but the serpent dodged with unnatural speed. I drove it back, and as it coiled to strike once more, I readied my weapon. The snake flew at me once again. This time I stepped preemptively and swung. With one smooth, powerful strike, I took the serpent's head clean off.

I stood there, breathing hard. The decapitated viper glared at me with fiery eyes.

The voice called out, "It is defeated."

But in my dream, I somehow knew that didn't mean it was dead—or done with me.

SATAN WASN'T DONE with me after my jail-induced sobriety either. I stayed clean for a while, not even drinking, but one bad breakup was all it took to get me back to liquor, meth, and crime.

Like many addicts, my relapse took me deeper than I had ever gone before. I started hanging out with guys that even my brother Paul warned me to stay away from. One of these was Hector. He was a real gang member, born and bred in Santa Cruz, not a wannabe. Stocky and short, he was a guy who didn't need tattoos or facial hair to let the world know they'd better not mess with him. His whole persona oozed that coolness, and he backed it up with a sharp criminal intelligence. He wasn't a drug dealer who was hooked and trying to get a constant supply, like Paul and I had been; Hector was the guy who taxed every drug transaction on his turf. Where most guys in the trade are either respected or feared, Hector had earned both emotions from everyone who knew him.

And in 2003, we were inseparable.

I shut the door and bolted it behind me.

"How was Rudy?" Hector asked.

"Fine," I answered, impatient to get to the meth I'd

bought from my old roommate. It had been too long since my last hit, and I was aching for my high. I cleared a space on the coffee table and took out the bag I'd bought from Rudy and started smoking it.

The meth burned up quickly, as if it evaporated into thin air. That was a bad sign.

The buzz I felt was about the same one might feel after drinking a Mr. Pibb. This wasn't tolerance; this was cut dope—drugs that had been mixed with other, inert substances to make the grams stretch longer. It's basically cheating, but of course you can't call the cops over it. The underworld has their own enforcers of fairness. And in Santa Cruz, one of the most feared of those enforcers was Hector.

When he came back in the room, I said, "Dude, Rudy's meth is super weak. I think he's cutting it."

Hector's features hardened dangerously, and he muttered dark curses under his breath. Then he locked eyes with me. "No one does that to my friends. Let's go over there and get what you paid for!"

My eyes widened. "What?" I didn't want to confront a friend—not like this, anyway. But it was Hector's bread and butter. "I don't know, Hector," I tried to protest. "It's not that big a deal—"

"It is to me. He's gonna sell meth on the Westside, he's gonna do it by *my* rules. How much did you buy?"

I told him I'd paid ninety bucks for what I got. Hector cursed in fury. "We're going *now.*"

I felt like a surfer being pushed along by a wave—a surfer who was barely hanging on. I followed Hector out the door and drove us to Rudy's place. He pounded on Rudy's door with his fist.

Rudy answered. He was a decent-size guy—a former pro surfer, in fact—with a good build, sun-bleached hair, and bronzed skin. The fact that he stood a head taller than Hector didn't stop my Latino friend for a millisecond.

"Just what do you think you're doing?"

Rudy retreated back a step, caught off guard by Hector's fury, and Hector immediately advanced to fill the space.

"You been selling weak meth to Danny."

"No, Hector, you know I'd never—"

"Don't you lie to me! I been on these streets my whole life. I know cut meth when I see it."

"I—I didn't mean—" Rudy backed up farther, and Hector kept advancing, finger in the bigger man's chest. I cautiously stepped through the doorway and spied a pair of girls on the couch, silent and wide eyed. Other people were there as well, and they were all freaked out.

"It ain't cool of you to rip off my friends. 'Cause, see, I'll find out about it. And then I'll be upset with you, just like I am right now. Where's your stash?"

"What?"

"You show me where your stash is right now, and we're gonna make this right. 'Cause you are gonna make this right for me, ain't you, Rudy?"

"Uh, yeah, sure. This way."

He took us to the next room and pulled out his stash from its hiding place. He fumbled with the bags, dropping some and picking them back up. His eyes kept darting back to Hector's left hand, which was resting almost casually in his pants pocket. Like everyone else in our world, Rudy knew that Hector preferred knives.

"Now you're going to give Danny what he paid for," Hector said.

Rudy nodded and measured out the meth. He zipped the bag up and handed it to Hector. Hector inspected it, then, satisfied, handed it to me. I put it in my pocket without a word.

"Good," Hector said. "Now the interest."

"What?" Rudy asked, confused.

Hector snatched another bag of meth from the stash. "This is for our trouble. It's an apology from you to me for what you did. Got that?"

It wasn't really a question, but Rudy answered it anyway. "Yeah. Sorry, Hector. Won't happen again."

"It better not, or this will be a pleasant visit compared to next time. Come on, Danny."

We left Rudy standing in that room with his significantly reduced stash, and I followed Hector past the terrified girls on the couch and back out the front door.

I kept quiet on the way back home. I don't like getting ripped off any more than the next person, but something about Hector's way of putting it "right" felt incredibly *wrong*. I wasn't going to say that to him, of course.

We went back to my studio apartment, and after a little while, I fell asleep—which shows just how weak that meth really was. I woke up to Hector shaking my shoulder. "Dude, someone's messing with your car!"

"What?" I got up and put my shoes on. We went outside and witnessed automotive vengeance. My car's windows were busted, and one of the tires was on fire.

Hector muttered a string of dark obscenities.

As the flames crackled on my car's tire, a flame of my own began rising up inside me. "Come on out, you cowards!" I screamed into the night. "You want a piece of me? Come and get it!"

The only answer in the still night air was a *pop* as my tire finally deflated.

MY PHONE BUZZED. I hesitated, then answered it. "Hello?"

"Danny?"

"Yeah."

"It's Kelly." Kelly was the kindest, most helpful person you would never expect an addict like me to have met. She ran in our circles yet seemed aloof from them, and from so many of the problems that hounded people like me. She also could've been a model: blonde haired, not too short and not too tall, with kind eyes and perfect proportions. Many men were interested in her, myself included.

"I hear things aren't going so well for you right now," she said.

"You could say that." The days since my confrontation with Rudy and the subsequent vandalization of my car had been the most stressful I'd ever known. Hector had escaped all consequences, of course, since no one could touch him. But they could touch me, and apparently I was the next best thing. "There's a contract out on me, Kelly. Someone's willing to pay good money to make me stop breathing." I'd been carrying a steak knife with me whenever I went outside. Meth makes one paranoid; adding real paranoia on top of that was not a healthy combination. I hadn't slept much the past several days.

"I know," Kelly said softly. "That's why I called."

That had not been what I'd expected to hear.

"I know some people who might be able to protect you," she continued. "Why don't you come up and visit me? You can meet them; we can figure out what to do."

Kelly lived about two hours away. And she was inviting *me* to come see *her.* There was only one answer. "Sounds great!" I said, trying to not sound *too* enthusiastic.

"Okay, I'll see you soon," she said.

"Yeah, definitely." I hung up and immediately got ready to go.

My brother Paul drove me out to Kelly's place. He was not exactly enthusiastic about it, though.

"All I'm saying is that if something were to happen, I'm too far away to help," Paul said, concerned as always for my safety.

"I don't think it'll be a problem," I said. "I don't think Rudy or anyone else is going to drive all the way out here."

"Not if they don't have to," Paul said darkly.

"What does that mean?" I asked.

"Did it ever cross your mind that this might be part of their plan? Get you far enough outside the city that they can do whatever they want, and no one's around to help you." He looked at me. "I'd never forgive myself if that happened."

With all the paranoia that comes from meth use, the thought *had* crossed my mind—but I'd dismissed it as too unlikely. Kelly wasn't like the people who were after me. Not only did she have nothing to gain, but it didn't feel right that she would wish me harm.

"I think her friends can help me," I said.

"Do you even know who they are?" Paul asked.

"No," I said, "but I trust Kelly.

Kelly looked as radiant as ever when Paul dropped me off at her work. I'd tried to make myself a little more presentable, but sleeplessness leaves signs you can't hide.

"Danny, I'm so glad you're here!" she said, giving me a warm embrace.

I enjoyed the hug, and when she pulled away, I said, "Thanks for inviting me up here. When do I meet your friends?"

She looked me up and down, sympathy and concern in her eyes. "After you get some sleep," she said.

And sleep I did. By the time I made up my slumber deficit, I was sober as well.

Once my mind was clear and my body refreshed, I met Kelly's friends. They were some of the most hard-core people I have ever met in my life, and the less said about that meeting, the better. Suffice it to say that they were very effective in convincing everyone in Santa Cruz that they'd better not touch me—and from then on, no one did.

But even this miraculous intervention didn't change the course of my life. After Kelly drove me back home, I fell into my same old habits. Only this time, I didn't have much of a circle of friends to share them with. Everyone knew not to touch me, but that didn't mean they had to keep my company. And many of my old friends didn't. I'd lost their trust and respect, and they were not inclined to give me a chance to win it back. I sought escape from my humiliation by chasing the next chemical high.

A few weeks later, Kelly called me again.

"How are you doing, Danny?"

"I'm okay."

"No one's trying to hurt you anymore, are they?"

"No, no, your friends took care of that really well. No one's tried anything."

"How are you sleeping?"

I paused. "Not so great."

"You're taking care of yourself, aren't you? The way we talked about?"

"Not really."

"Danny, are you still using meth after you *promised* me you wouldn't anymore?"

I didn't want to lie to her, so I didn't. "Yes," I said. "I am."

She nearly exploded. "I can't believe this! After everything I've done, all the favors I called in—how could you do this to me?"

There was no good answer, but I tried anyway. "Kelly, I'm sorry. I . . . it's been really tough . . ."

"Tougher than where you were before?" she taunted.

"No, but—"

"Then why are you still using? Why did you lie to me?"

"I didn't! I just—"

The line went dead.

I tried to call her back. She didn't answer. She didn't answer later that day, or the next day either. I slowly realized that I'd screwed up the one relationship keeping me in Santa Cruz. There was nothing left for me in California. I needed to be somewhere else.

I called up my brother John, who was living in Arkansas, and he agreed to let me move out there with him. I wasted no time in making the arrangements.

While I was packing up, Hector came over to see me. He was probably the only person left in Santa Cruz, besides my brother Paul, who would miss me once I left.

"You sure you gotta go, man?"

I put another pair of shorts into my duffel bag. "Yeah. I'm sure."

"Won't be the same without you."

I shrugged. "It's not like I've really been doing much here the last few weeks anyway."

Hector had nothing to say to that. Finally, he said, "You want some meth before you go?"

My body did want it, but in part, that's what I was moving to get away from. I wouldn't be starting much of a new life in Arkansas if I went there high as a kite. "No," I said. "Thanks."

Hector couldn't believe his ears. "Are you sure, man?" He'd never seen me turn down meth before.

"Yes, I am."

"No way. You gotta be messin' with me. Mr. Always-Takes-Another-Hit doesn't want his meth?"

"I don't."

"No, man, I don't believe you. You gotta want some."

"I really don't, Hector. I'm telling the truth."

He took a bag out of his pocket and swung it like a pendulum. "Come on, man. Free of charge. It's the least I can do."

Nope. Not again. I was going to be clean. I was going to get off it.

"I'll just leave it here on the table for you," Hector said. "Call me if you want some more."

"You leave it there, it'll just get wasted," I warned him. "I won't use it."

Hector shrugged. "Do whatever you want with it. See you later, Danny."

"Goodbye, Hector," I said.

And he was gone.

I went to the table and picked up the bag he'd left. It was high-quality merchandise. The temptation was still there. I knew how it would make me feel if I took it. But this was the stuff that had cost me my friendship with Kelly. This simple white powder had cost me my home, my friends, jobs, and my peace of mind. And I knew if I kept staring at it, I would use it again, and then it would take even more away from me.

No, I thought. *Not this time.* I marched to the bathroom, opened the bag, and flushed every bit of it down the toilet.

"No more addictions," I whispered to myself. And then, to prove the point, I collected every scrap of porn I owned and threw it all in the trash.

69

I stood in my nearly empty room, breathing hard, as though I'd just run a marathon or lifted weights. And yet I felt light and energized. Something had begun in that room, with those two small yet momentous decisions. I didn't know then what the outcome would be—at best, I had a desire to hope for it—but that moment was the beginning of a transformation that would last for years, culminating in a thirty-day fast in the Washington wilderness.

I AWOKE DURING THE second week of my fast to chattering teeth and what felt like lightning arcing up and down my spine. I'd dismissed the growing discomfort in my old back injuries as a result of going without food for so long, but now I was forced to confront reality: my fragile back was not taking well to sleeping on the ground.

I cried out in pain as I sat up. My breath formed in front of me like smoke in the chilly air. I tried not to whimper as I crawled out of my tent. Pain stabbed down my sciatic nerve and into my right leg as I tried to straighten up. Frost sparkled on the ground.

Trying to go about my morning ritual was excruciating. Instead of walking to the bathroom—located a mere hundred yards away—I drove. Getting into and out of the driver's seat felt like getting kicked in the pelvis with steel-toed boots. My body was no longer circulating blood as efficiently, and warming up my hands took more energy than I could spare.

By midday, I confessed to myself that something was going to have to change or I wasn't going to make it another night, let alone till I had completed my goal.

And God had promised me victory. I *had* to stick this through.

I dug my cell phone out of my car and fumbled through my contacts. Finally, I found the one I wanted and pressed Dial.

The phone rang three times before my wife, Sally, answered. "Danny," she said, "are you okay?"

"Yes and no," I answered. "I'm safe and everything, but my back has started acting up again."

"Oh." She'd recently endured a year of me being off my feet after major back surgery. Truth be told, I wasn't fully recovered yet. And my downtime had been hard on her. It was part of the reason she'd supported my cockamamy idea to camp out in the wilderness for a month or longer. "Are you coming home already?" she asked.

"I don't want to come home just yet," I replied. "But I need your help if I'm going to stay out here any longer."

"What do you need?"

"The ground under the tent is killing my back. Plus, it's getting pretty chilly up here," I added as my breath sailed away in a cloud. "The back seats in the Jeep fold down, right?"

"Yes."

"Can you come and switch cars with me?"

Silence hung over the line for several seconds. I squeezed my eyes shut and prayed. The Grand Cherokee was her favorite car. I realized with a shock that the success of my fast might depend on whether my wife was willing to give up her car to me for the next few weeks. *Please let her say yes, God. I still need to be here.*

After a several-second eternity, Sally said, "Sure. I'll be there in a couple hours."

I exhaled in relief. "Thank you, Sally."

"See you soon."

Sally was punctual, as usual. I felt my body relax when the Grand Cherokee appeared around the bend of the road. I would be able to stay here after all.

Sally pulled up next to my Chrysler and exited her SUV. She looked exactly as she had two weeks ago: mid length blonde hair and plucked eyebrows over smile lines and sun-tanned skin. Her Reiki energy healing crystal hung from a silver necklace. She was eleven years older than me, but we'd made our marriage work. So far.

"How are you doing?" she asked.

"I'll be doing better now. Thanks for bringing me the Grand Cherokee. I think I'll sleep a lot better in the back."

Sally surveyed my campsite, then looked at me. I recognized a strangely familiar hardness in her eyes—one that reminded me of the day we'd first met.

I'D FIRST MET SALLY when I was working as a trainer at a local gym. I remember her coming in, an attractive older woman with a look of steely determination on her face. I'd seen her there before, so when she approached the desk, I said, "Welcome back."

"Thanks," she said. "I'd like to get my membership back, please."

"Certainly," I said, clicking to the right screen on the computer. "I didn't realize you'd canceled."

"Yes." She gave me her information, and I located the old record.

"It says here you only discontinued a few weeks ago. Couldn't stay away?" I asked with a grin.

"Actually, I was going to move away to get married. It didn't work out."

"Oh," I said, embarrassed. "I'm sorry."

"Don't be," she said, holding her chin up high. "It's for the best."

I finalized her membership renewal, and she immediately went to one of the treadmills. The next day, she was back again. And the next—always running, even though on a treadmill you never get anywhere. Part of me wondered if she was running from her past or toward her future. She always wore that same mask of determination and resolve. Wherever she was going, she was serious about it—but I knew better than most how much pain could hide behind a mask like hers.

The fourth day, I decided to say something to her. I walked up to her while she was on the treadmill and said, "I know you don't know me, but you're probably going through a lot. If you need someone to talk to, you can talk to me."

She looked shocked for a second, but then a tender smile creased her lips. "Thank you," she said. "I will."

I smiled and walked away.

A few days later, Sally sought me out. I greeted her warmly and asked if there was anything I could help her with (I was still an employee, after all).

"Yes," she said. She seemed a little nervous.

I nodded for her to continue. She took a deep breath and said, "There's a half marathon coming up that I'd like to run. Could you help me train for it?" She watched for my reaction, biting her lip expectantly.

I grinned. "Of course I can."

That was the one bright spot in my job that day. Things

had been deteriorating between me and the owner for a while, and that afternoon, my employment was officially terminated. I didn't see Sally again until I came back to collect my final paycheck.

She came up to me as soon as I walked in the door. "Danny!" she called. "I've been looking for you."

"You almost didn't find me," I said. "I don't work here anymore."

"Yes, I heard what happened. I'm so sorry."

I shrugged. "It's been a long time coming," I said. I really did *not* want to discuss the details with her. "I'm sorry I won't be training you for your half marathon."

"Actually, I wanted to talk with you about that," she said.

At my questioning glance, she continued, "I'd still like you to train me—as a personal trainer, not through the gym."

That had not been the reaction I'd expected. I had been training on the side for a couple of months at that point, but there was something else in her expression—an unspoken invitation behind the smile in her eyes.

"Yes," I said. "I'd like that. I'd like that a lot."

"Good!"

Training led to dating, and dating leads to marriage. But at that juncture when a serious relationship prompts discussions of "What's next?" I felt a hesitation I could not explain.

From the outside, our relationship looked amazing. We were both fit and healthy, we got along great, and we had many things in common. We seldom argued. Everyone thought we were the perfect couple. But I had an inexplicable intuition that something wasn't quite right in our relationship.

I brought it up only one time. We were sitting on her couch after a date that had gone just as flawlessly as all our others when I looked at her and said, "Sally, do you ever feel like something is . . . off between us?"

Her brow furrowed. "No. What do you mean?"

"It's hard to explain. I can't really put my finger on it. I'm just not sure if it's right."

She turned toward me and looked me in the eye. "Danny, are you breaking up with me?"

"I'm just trying to figure out if there's any reason we shouldn't be together—"

"You're trying to find reasons to *not* be with me?"

"That's not what I meant!" But it was too late. She started crying. I tried to comfort her, but she shook me off.

"If you're going to end this, I wish you'd just say so!"

Now it was my turn to start panicking. "I'm not breaking up with you!"

"Oh, really? You're just going to tell me that you think

there's something wrong with us—something you can't even *say* what it is—but you're not breaking up with me?"

"That came out wrong. I'm sorry." I was grasping at straws, but sometimes that's all you can think to do.

"Look, Danny," she said, trying to regain her composure, "I care about you. I love you. I think that's enough for any relationship. Don't you?"

I didn't really know, but I said yes anyway. And I never did at that time find an articulable reason why our relationship *shouldn't* continue to progress to marriage, so eventually I overrode my intuition and proposed.

Sally accepted.

At first, everything fell together nicely. We opened a gym together where we took a holistic approach to health and fitness. Sally offered mental and emotional counseling to our clients so that they could gain the stability they needed to be successful in their dietary and fitness goals, which I coached them to achieve. We offered massage therapy, yoga, tai chi, and meditation in addition to regular weights and cardio, and we gained a reputation as a gym that helped post-gastric bypass patients develop healthier lifestyles.

But it didn't last. In less than a year, the economy conspired with our location and other factors and forced us to close. Our marriage survived that, though if I was honest with myself, we'd been drifting slowly apart ever since.

NOW, IN MY CAMPSITE, Sally was looking at me more like I was a friend she was doing a favor for than like I was her husband. So when she asked me, "How much longer do you think you'll be out here?" she might have been asking, *When do I get my SUV back?*

"I don't know," I said. "I'm not done out here yet."

She looked like she was about to say something else, but then she closed her mouth and nodded. "Take all the time you need."

We exchanged a quick peck on the cheek, and then she slipped into my Chrysler 300. Before she shut the door, she looked up at me and said, "Danny?"

"Yes?"

"Take care of yourself out here."

"I will," I promised.

She smiled, shut the car door, and drove away.

———————◆———————

SALLY'S VISIT GOT ME thinking about the other women who'd come and gone in my life. A part of me had always been terrified of girls. As I thought about it, I traced my feelings back to an incident that occurred when I was about five years old.

My parents were friends with a family who had a daughter my same age. When our parents got together (which was frequently), she and I would play. We became as good of friends as five-year-olds are capable of being—that is to say, we got comfortable around each other.

During one such visit, as we were playing in my room, one of us repeated something we'd heard about the physical differences between boys and girls. I don't remember whose idea it was, but with childish curiosity, we decided to find out what those differences were. After all, we each had what the other hadn't seen—and that's as far as a five-year-old's thought process goes. We ended up underneath my bed, completely naked, exploring each other's bodies, when my mother walked in.

"What are you two doing under there?"

"Nothing." Which was obviously not true, but we didn't have a word to describe what we were doing.

"Come out of there!"

So we did. At that point, we were more afraid of being punished for disobeying my mother than for taking our clothes off. We maybe had an inkling that our parents wouldn't like it—which is why we hid—but we had no concept of morality or chastity. We were five years old. We didn't even comprehend the difference between right and wrong, and we couldn't really be held accountable for our actions.

I wish my mother had remembered that when she saw us standing there in the nude. Instead, shocked and, I'm sure, socially mortified, she went livid and started giving me the most painful, humiliating spanking I ever experienced. This brought my friend's mother into the room, and she dealt out her own punishment to her naked daughter.

As the blows landed on my unprotected bottom, what had started out as curiosity and play turned into fear and anguish. It taught me a lesson my mother did not intend: that females equaled pain. (This was reinforced again years later, when my mom divorced my dad.)

I reflected on this incident while I laid down the back seat of Sally's SUV—my bed until I finished my fast. Could all my troubles with women have been caused by this single episode of trauma? Certainly it affected my outlook on women. In general, I was too scared to talk to them at all unless I'd had a few drinks first. Pornography and masturbation had seemed a "safer" path to pleasure because they offered no possibility to physically get hurt. But no. Other guys have had mothers even less perfect than mine—ones who were truly, consistently abusive, which mine wasn't—and they hadn't made the same mistakes that I had. Even with the consequences of this event in mind, the decisions I'd made in my life were my own. I couldn't blame my mother for them.

After all, she hadn't been a major presence in my life for years when I had my first serious relationship, with a girl named Tracy. We'd met as coworkers at a local grocery store. She had luxurious black hair, dark eyes, and a natural skin tone that most white girls would kill for. I'd found her attractive since day one, but it wasn't until months later, in late 2000, that I ran into her walking on a gravel path by the beach and asked her out.

Unfortunately, this was right about the time when my friends and I began substituting our cocaine habit for a meth addiction. Relationships are hard enough when one party has issues like substance abuse or mental illness. When both sides have one or more of these issues, life becomes impossible. That's what Tracy and I learned as I introduced her to my new chemical of choice. A part of me knew—and even said, at the time—that this drug could potentially ruin our lives. But I didn't have the strength to listen to myself back then.

And it did. Before long, I was jobless and homeless, crashing at friends' houses or, when I could afford it, the occasional hotel. Tracy managed to stay more steadily employed, so she became the one financially supporting our addiction.

One night, Tracy's mother hosted a party, and I made her whole family chiles rellenos. They were a big hit. Afterward, as I was doing the dishes to help clean up, Tracy's mom came up to me and said, "You're the perfect man—you cook *and* clean!"

I smiled and tried not to blush, but earning points in your girlfriend's mom's eyes is never a bad thing. "Aw, it's nothing," I said.

"Don't be so modest! It's a rare sight, in my experience," she declared, shooting a significant glance at her ex-husband, Tracy's father. (Even though they were divorced, he was frequently around to spend time with Tracy.) He just shrugged. Then, she added quietly, "Tracy tells me you've been having trouble finding a place to live."

I nodded, now ashamed in addition to embarrassed.

"If you keep doing things like this," she said, motioning toward the soapy dishes, "you could move in here, you know."

I hadn't considered that as a possibility before. But Tracy liked the idea, and so I did.

Good things can happen to a person who's suffering from a drug addiction, but the addiction tends to ensure that those good things don't last. Tracy and I continued our meth usage in secret, but we couldn't hide all its effects from her parents. As we used more heavily, Tracy's hyperactivity got significantly worse. She began snapping at her father and ignoring her mother. One day, as I was on my way out the door to meet with a friend, they pulled me aside.

"Danny," Tracy's mother said, "we're worried about

Tracy. She hasn't been acting like herself lately. You've noticed, haven't you?"

"Yeah," I said.

"What's wrong with her?"

"What do you mean?"

At this point her father interrupted. "Is she on some kind of drugs?" he asked.

"We want to help if we can," her mother added.

I thought about Tracy, who was sitting in her room, coming down from a high because she needed to go to work later. She'd been able to stay employed better than I had, but at the rate we were using, it wouldn't last. My life was in shambles, but hers wasn't yet, and it didn't need to be. I thought about lying like we had before, but with them already suspecting the truth, I didn't think I could be convincing. And something about that dangled promise of help pushed me over the edge and into confession.

"It's methamphetamines," I said, and her mother gasped. Her father's face simply hardened. "We're both on it. We want to get off, but it's so hard. So anything you could do . . ."

"I see," said her mother.

A honk sounded from outside. "I kinda gotta go," I said, motioning toward the noise.

"We'll talk about this when you get back," she said.

87

When I did come back, several hours later, I found Tracy's mother on the front porch waiting for me, next to a pile of my clothes sitting on the front lawn. "Danny, I think it's time you found another place to live. I hope you understand."

"Uh . . ."

"We had a long talk with Tracy, and we don't think you being here is a good influence on her. As her parents, it's our job to keep her safe."

"Sure," I said, looking back and forth between her and the pile of clothing. My brain was struggling to process what was happening.

"Sorry about this," she said with an apologetic wince and a nod toward the pile. "When I talked to Tracy, she got upset and . . ." She shrugged, then added, "Tracy wants to talk with you."

"Okay."

She went inside, and a moment later, Tracy came out, slamming the door behind her. "I can't believe you told my parents! I can't believe you did that to me! What were you thinking?"

"Tracy, we need to get clean. We've talked about this. They started guessing, and I thought maybe they could help us."

"Well, they're 'helping' by throwing you out! Is that what you wanted?"

"No."

"What did you think was going to happen? I told you that I wasn't ready to tell them yet—because I knew they'd react like this! Why can't you listen to me?"

"I did, but—"

"*Sure* you did! You told them what I told you *not* to! What makes you think you have the right to speak for me?"

"I wasn't trying to speak for you!"

"Well, you did, and look what it got us!"

Her accusation hung in the air as I contemplated the pile of clothing.

When Tracy spoke again, there was a choke in her voice. "Take your stuff and go!"

A few weeks later, she said we needed to talk, so we met in person. What she said was not what I expected.

"Danny, I'm pregnant."

"Say that again, Tracy?" I was so shocked I was sure I'd heard wrong. But I hadn't.

"I'm pregnant."

"Are you sure?"

"Yeah, I'm sure." We need to talk about what we're going

to do." I was torn between wanting to sit down and wanting to pace around in nervous agitation. But mostly, I was terrified. *Am I ready to be a father?* I asked myself. The answer to that was obvious. I was unemployed, homeless, and addicted to methamphetamines—and Tracy was addicted too. No, I was not ready. *What kind of life would that child even have?* I asked myself. When I thought of what Tracy and I could provide, I shuddered.

"I'm not ready to be a parent," I said.

"Me either," Tracy replied. "Maybe I should get an abortion."

"Well, hold on, let's think of options. Yeah, we need options. We need to think of all the possibilities and then eliminate the ones that won't work. We're not ready to be parents, so that's out, right?"

I could hear relief in her voice as she said, "Yes, I think so."

"Could your parents take care of the baby?"

"I don't know. They're kind of old, and they're still upset at us."

"Okay, do we know anyone else who would want to adopt it?"

Silence.

I didn't know anyone like that either.

"I guess we could put it up through an agency," Tracy said, "but what if I actually have it and I can't give it up?"

"I don't know," I admitted. "And even putting it up for adoption through an agency doesn't guarantee it a good life or anything." I'd heard horror stories of foster care that were even worse than what I imagined Tracy and I could provide. I certainly didn't want to put a kid through *that.*

"No, I guess not. Plus, I'd have to deal with being pregnant for the next nine months. I threw up this morning. It sucked. I don't want to go through that for the next three months or longer. I mean, what if I can't go in to work, and they fire me? Or what if there's some kind of complication? I don't have insurance."

I didn't, either, being unemployed, and Tracy was too old to be covered by her parents' plan.

"If I had the baby, it would cost thousands of dollars that I don't have," Tracy said.

"I'm sure your parents would help out—"

"You will *not* tell my parents about this! We are *not* doing that again."

"Okay, okay," I said, cowed by recent experience. "They won't hear a word from me."

"An abortion at this point's only a few hundred. I can afford that."

The word *abortion* hung in the air like smoke in a bar. I'd been taught as a child that abortion was wrong, and I didn't feel good about considering it now. But try as I might, I couldn't think of any other option that sounded possible.

"I can't think of anything else we could do," I confessed.

"Will you give me a ride to the clinic?" Tracy asked. "My parents can think it's a date . . ."

"That's some kind of date," I muttered. "Yeah, sure. I'll borrow a car from someone."

That person eventually flaked, and I wasn't able to keep my promise to Tracy. She got even more upset at me after that, but about that time I decided to move down to San Clemente to move in with my dad and stepmother just to get a roof over my head. My brother Paul drove me down, and I was a wreck the entire seven-hour drive. I cried because I was leaving Tracy, because of the abortion she was getting without me there, and because I was absolutely sure, in my drug-altered mind, that she was already sleeping with one or more of my friends.

The thoughts didn't end when I reached Southern California. Images of her being with other guys so tormented me that I couldn't keep a job there either. At times, I "did curse God, and wish to die" (Mormon 2:14), literally shoving my middle fingers toward heaven as I screamed. And certainly Tracy did rebound to her next relationship much faster than I did. My experience with her solidified a bitterness toward women that lasted for two whole years, until, after I got out of

Camp Snoopy, some mutual friends introduced me to a girl named Helen.

Helen had blonde hair, brown eyes, full lips, and a body she knew was sexy. Unlike Tracy, she didn't have substance abuse problems. She drank only in moderation and never did hard drugs. Having just gotten sober in jail, I was trying to keep myself clean, and I was finally over Tracy enough to be excited at the possibility of having a sober relationship. Without the drugs interfering, I thought, maybe things could work out.

Helen and I hit it off immediately. She was a fun girl with a good heart. We hung out at our mutual friend's house and watched movies right after I was released for good behavior. We laughed and joked a lot, and we had serious, respectful discussions about our feelings as they began to grow. And she loved my cooking.

But I'd come back to Santa Cruz only to do my time, and then I needed to go back to my dad's house in San Clemente. So I went back, but Helen and I kept in touch over the phone.

"I miss you, Danny."

"I know, Helen. I miss you too."

"Some friends are having a barbecue tonight. I wish you were going to be there with me."

"So do I."

"How are you doing down there?"

"Working with my dad. Saving money. It's all right, just . . . lonely."

"I'm lonely too."

Our conversations went on like that for a few weeks, until one night Helen said, "I want you to move back up here. So we can be together."

My heart fluttered with excitement. I wanted to be with Helen more than anything. But there was one problem. "I don't think I have enough money to afford to move."

"I'll come down and drive you up. What kind of girlfriend would I be if I didn't do everything I could to help us be together?"

A little voice in the back of my head reminded me that Santa Cruz was where I had gotten heavily into drugs, and all my friends who were using were still there. But I'd been clean for months now, ever since getting sober in jail. *I have a handle on it*, I told myself. And so I agreed.

Helen was as good as her word. She made the seven-hour drive down to pick me up, then turned around and drove me back north. I rented a little studio apartment in the back of a friend's house. I could tell from the smell in the air that they were all still doing meth, but I told myself that the studio was separated enough that it wouldn't be a problem. Besides, I was here to be with Helen. She was more exciting and important than getting high.

And for two months, that was true. Although it was my

first real sober relationship, I never felt shy or awkward around Helen, like I usually did around beautiful women. I felt comfortable. I could be myself, and she enjoyed it. I even met her family, and we got along great. Everything seemed to be going perfectly.

Then, one night, after a fun couple of hours hanging out at a friend's house, Helen was a bit quieter than usual as she drove me back to my studio. I wasn't worried; I looked out the passenger window at homes and streetlights passing us by. Helen's voice broke me out of my reverie.

"Danny, I really like you."

"That's good," I said, "because I really like you too."

The fact that she didn't return my smile was the first sign of trouble that my brain recognized.

"I know," she said, "but I don't feel like we should be together anymore."

I was blindsided. "W-what?" was all I could manage to stammer out.

She shook her head sadly. "I just don't think it's going to work out between us. But I want us to stay friends."

"Whoa, whoa, whoa—you're breaking up with me?" I'd had *no* inkling that this was coming.

"I think I need to."

"But *why?*"

She didn't have a real answer to that. She enjoyed our time together, and she thought I was a good person, but apparently all that wasn't enough.

"Please," I pleaded, "give me a chance! Tell me something to change, and I can do it—"

"It's not that I want you to change, Danny. I think you're a great guy how you are. I just don't think that *we're* right for each other."

"What's the difference?"

She ignored my question. "I do want us to stay friends," she insisted. "Just not more than that."

She put the car in park, and I realized we'd arrived at my place. I stared at her.

She stared back. "Well?" she asked.

"I moved out here to be more than friends with you. I uprooted my entire *life* so we could be together, because *you* asked me to. You said you wanted this, and now you're dropping me like a bad habit?"

"I'm sorry, but—"

"No. No, *sorry* isn't going to cut it. This is, like, seven levels of screwed up, Helen. I can't just settle for the friend zone. If we're not dating, then we can't be friends."

She looked sad, but I could see my words were not convincing her to change her mind. "I'm not doing this to try to hurt you. I swear. I know it will hurt, but that's not my intention."

"Well, you have a pretty messed-up way of showing it." I got out of my seat and stood by the side of the car, holding the door open. "I don't know what you thought you were doing, but encouraging me to move out here to be with you, then dumping me like this . . . Do you know what this is? It's cruel. That's what it is. It's cruel, and it's wrong."

"Danny, I—"

I slammed the door shut and stormed away. I wasn't interested in hearing anything else. In that moment, all I wanted was something to dull the tearing anguish in my chest. And my tormented brain remembered exactly where I could find that numbness.

I asked a friend for a shot of Jack Daniel's. One shot led to another. Later that night, in a drunken desperation to think of how I'd move forward, I got some meth from one of my roommates.

From there, it was less than a year until Hector would be getting me in trouble with Rudy.

NOW, SITTING ON A park bench by a stream in Washington State, watching a flock of birds fly south overhead, I reflected on these women from my past. There was blame enough on all sides, to be sure, but the blame I saw most clearly was my own. Helen may have broken my heart—and I still wasn't entirely sure why—but she hadn't forced the booze past my lips or the meth into my lungs. I'd done those things to myself, in a bad reaction to what she'd done. The responsibility for those choices was mine, not hers.

Same with Tracy—I had betrayed her confidence to her parents. The fact that I'd done it with good intentions didn't absolve me of responsibility, especially since she wouldn't have been on meth if I hadn't introduced her to it. I still didn't know for sure if I'd caused her pregnancy, but I'd certainly been acting in such a way with her that it could have been mine. And what *I* did was on *me*, even if someone else went along with it.

And Sally. Had I been the best husband to her over the years? Sitting there with no one to lie to but myself, I had to admit the truth: I could have done better. My initial hesitance about our relationship had colored my actions ever since, and I'd always kept a part of myself held back in reserve, unwilling to commit as fully as I knew a husband ought. And though we never spoke about it, I was sure some subconscious part of her had recognized that too.

In all these relationships—and others—I had sinned, and I had no one I could blame for it but myself.

I walked, slowly, back to Sally's SUV, weighed down by more than just the emptiness in my stomach. Guilt and regret felt like twin shackles encircling my feet, making each step drag. But I made it to the Grand Cherokee and drove back to my campsite. Luckily, the weight I felt did not translate into a lead foot.

That night, as I was sleeping in the lowered back seats, I dreamed a third time. A naked woman approached me. She had tan skin, long dark hair, and seductive, almost hypnotizing eyes that scanned me from head to toe, appraising me.

"Hello, Danny," she purred with obvious interest. Her voice seemed to echo all my past lovers. "I've been waiting for you." Her desire was as obvious as it was intoxicating, but even in my dream, I knew something about this wasn't right. I kept myself rooted to the spot.

"You can have me if you want me," she said. "All you have to do is sell your soul and I'm yours."

I heard a slithering behind me, and I realized that the serpent might not have been visible this time, but he was there, and he was tempting me. This was a test—one of the hardest ones I'd yet faced. I could feel my body responding, lustful with desire, as I had trained it to for so many years of one-night stands, pornography, and other sexual addictions throughout my life. But my fast had strengthened me. I hadn't given in to my body's appetite for food for twenty days, and I wasn't going to give in to this sexual appetite either. And in that moment, I realized that they really were the same when it came down to it. All the things our bodies want—from food to sex to drugs to entertainment—are things that we, as those who control our bodies, can choose whether or not to provide. The urge may be strong, even seemingly irresistible, but at the end, *we* have control until we choose to surrender it to addictions of any sort. My fast had taught me this, though not, till then, in words.

So I resisted. I looked into her seductive eyes and firmly said, "My soul belongs to God, and God only."

Her lips turned down into a pouty frown. Her eyes began to glisten.

But I would not let her guilt me into sinning. "No," I said. "You have no power over me. Be gone, Satan."

The woman's eyes flashed. She bared her teeth and hissed, but she couldn't touch me. Then she slowly withdrew, disappearing into the darkness.

I awoke breathing hard. My body shuddered as I tried to calm my racing heart. I remembered the story of Buddha, which I had studied a few months before. On his own path to enlightenment, he had also been tempted. Three women had come to seduce him, but he overcame their temptation.

Just as I now had.

My insides clenched in hunger pains. *How much longer can I last?* I wondered.

THE NEXT DAY, I was tempted yet again—this time by plain old hunger.

I had driven back to the scenic view with the park bench and stumbled over to sit on it. As I hung my head in weariness, my gaze focused in on a tuft of grass growing just a foot off to the side of my bench. It was so green and lush and full. Frost had melted into dew but not yet evaporated. The drops sparkled in the early-morning sunlight.

My insides churned with emptiness and longing. And I realized: that grass looked *good.* My mouth began to salivate.

A voice inside my head whispered, "Just eat one little blade of grass. Just one. Think how good it will feel to taste something on your tongue. Just one little blade won't hurt your fast."

It was Satan again, and I recognized him—and his lie. I had promised God a real fast. One blade of grass would have negated the whole experience—all the work and effort I'd suffered through so far, gone for a taste of something that wasn't even food. Just like that one shot of Jack Daniel's after Helen broke up with me ruined months of sobriety, so one little blade of grass could ruin the great venture I'd set out on here in Riverside State Park.

I remembered a verse in the Bible, from the story that had inspired my own fast out here: Jesus's forty-day fast and temptation in the Judean wilderness. "And the devil said unto him, If thou be the Son of God, command this stone that it be made bread. And Jesus answered him, saying, It is written, That man shall not live by bread alone, but by every word of God" (Luke 4:3-4).

I realized I had been leaning down toward that patch of grass, one hand extended. I pulled it back and sat up straight. I closed my eyes and felt the sunlight warm my face. "Nice try, Satan," I whispered, "but not this time."

I felt a comforting glow of victory—one that was just familiar enough for me to recognize. I recalled feeling it in 2003, just after I'd left Hector and his meth back in Santa Cruz and moved across the country to live with my brother John in Paragould, Arkansas.

THE SILVER-HAIRED LADY stopped her old Buick at the stop sign, saw me waiting on the corner to cross the street, and waved me forward with a smile. As I walked in front of her windshield, she waved again—a good old-fashioned southern gesture of greeting and goodwill.

It made me feel completely weird. I hurried across the street and kept making my way back to John's house. A couple walking their dog waved at me from across the street. And so did nearly every other lifetime resident of Paragould.

Why are they waving at me? I wondered. *I don't know them.*

Moving from Santa Cruz to the South was a major culture shock. Not only was the city a quarter of the size of where I had been living, but the people in it acted very differently. On the one hand, it was hard *not* to feel welcomed; on the other, it made me wonder what they all were after.

But that was the meth withdrawal talking. It had been only a week and a half since I'd thrown away Hector's meth and all my pornography and flown halfway across the country. But my brain didn't know that I was trying to start a new life; it was still expecting the next hit. I caught myself thinking things like, *Why are they being so nice? It's probably fake . . . but* why *are they doing it? What do they know about me?*

Meth takes a few days to work its way out of your system, but even when it's completely gone, its effects linger. The good people of Paragould were just extending traditional southern hospitality to me. But the chemical withdrawal prevented me from accepting that as the rational explanation.

At the house next door to my brother's, I slowed my pace. The neighbor was outside, sitting on the porch. That in itself was not unusual in this town, but there was something in his face that looked familiar. It was in the way his eyes darted back and forth, taking in each sight, and in the way his lips moved constantly, as if he were having a silent conversation with the empty air.

"Hey," I said.

His eyes focused and darted up and down as he took me in.

"You're new," he said.

"Yeah, I just moved in next door. John's my brother."

"I know John," he said. "Good neighbor. Nice guy. Doesn't bother people. Nice wife too." He seemed a little scatterbrained—just like I used to be when coming down from a hit. But it wasn't enough to be sure; some people are just naturally weird.

We exchanged names, and I asked, "So what do you do?"

"Odd jobs, a bit of construction."

He didn't seem to want to say anything more, so I said, "Well, you have a nice day." He murmured something noncommittal and went back to his voiceless whispering. I went up the steps to my brother's house and kept myself from looking back at the neighbor.

When John came home, I asked him about the man.

"Yeah, I think he is on something," John confirmed. "Probably meth, from what I've seen."

"Does he ever work?" I asked.

John shrugged. "Well, *I* do, so it's not like I'm home enough to tell if he's leaving for work every day."

With that, I got the strong suspicion that right next door to my brother, I had a supplier—if I wanted one. Our next-door neighbor was the small-town equivalent of one of Hector's goons. Again, that voice in the back of my head promised that I could figure everything out if I just had some of what this man could offer me. And if I ever needed more, he was only next door.

I screwed my eyes shut and shook my head. I had come out here to *escape* that lifestyle, not fall right back in it. I had to be strong. If I ever saw him again, I would just keep walking.

But that did nothing to calm the anxiousness in my mind.

That night, as I was lying in bed, trying to go to sleep, a face flashed before my eyes: Mary, Alan's girlfriend back in Santa Cruz. I'd hung out with both her and Alan quite a bit while I had been dating Helen and since she'd broken up with me. Mary was small, gorgeous, and half-Mexican—and if I ever had a "type," petite Mexican girl was it. But as I lay there, staring up at my ceiling and reviewing all our interactions together, it struck me how kind, gentle, loving, quiet, and humble Mary had always been. My drug-scarred mind began constructing an image of her on top of a pedestal: an ideal woman, the kind of person I wanted to be with. But I had never been with Mary, or really, with anyone even like her. Why not?

My mind came up with a rationalization: because I had never been good enough for her. I had always been using drugs, and it wasn't right for such a good, wonderful girl to be with a guy who was on drugs. I wasn't worthy of her yet.

That must be why I'm here, I thought. I needed to come out here to get clean so that I could become a man who was worthy of this Mary I'd constructed in my brain. With that in mind, the events of the past several years seemed to snap into focus. My friends hadn't really been out to get me after the incident with Hector and Rudy—it had all been an elaborate scheme to scare me into quitting. That's why Kelly's friends had been so effective—and why she'd been so upset when I'd fallen back into using. They were my friends. Of course they'd been doing it all for my own good.

Which meant that if I succeeded *this* time, I'd get the prize. Mary would choose a cleaned-up, reformed Danny, wouldn't she? Of course she would. She'd probably been waiting for this the whole time. I reviewed our conversations together, her looks at me, her smiles—yes, yes, it all made sense.

But I couldn't be clean for just a week or a month or even a year. No, no, that wouldn't do. It wouldn't be enough at all to prove I'd properly, fully reformed. Only then could I be worthy of her. Only then could I be sure that Mary would be with me.

The next day, I threw my cigarettes in the garbage. I quit cold turkey, and I was able to because I was convinced it's what Mary wanted me to do. I also called Alan. I told him it was because I wanted to hear how he was doing, but in reality, I wanted to know how she was doing even more.

What Alan told me should have been a shocker: "Mary's pregnant. We're going to have a baby."

"Wow," I said in reply. "Congratulations." But my brain was working feverishly to adapt this bit of information to my new worldview. If Mary and Alan had a baby together, then obviously Mary wouldn't end up with me. But since I was sure she was going to end up with me, that couldn't possibly be the case. No, the baby wasn't Alan's at all—it was mine. That would make it just that much more certain that Mary and I would be together.

The fact that I'd never had sex with Mary didn't stop that thought for a moment. The determined mind can always invent an explanation and decide to believe it's plausible.

The girl I'd had sex with most recently was Leslie. It hadn't been a real relationship, just a casual fling, but now it made more sense why Leslie would have wanted that—obviously, she had taken my sperm to impregnate Mary. At Mary's request, of course—after all, everything my friends had done was an elaborate scheme to get me clean so Mary and I could be together. Sending a surrogate sexual partner to steal sperm made perfect sense in that context.

Of course, all of this was true only inside my drug-altered, withdrawal-racked brain. None of it was true in the real world. But the way these thought processes led me to act did have real-world consequences, at least in my life. I became so convinced that Mary would call me, or just show up one day, that when she kept not calling and not appearing, I got stressed and made myself sick. And because I was still trying to live a lifestyle worthy of her, I didn't take alcohol to make my strep throat feel better or drugs to dull my earache away. I simply made myself endure—for Mary.

But the brain can endure only so many disappointed expectations before it cracks. Mine cracked on a rainy day when I had gone to the doctor's office seeking treatment for an ear infection. Yet again, Mary had neither come nor called nor even sent a letter. And since I had no insurance, the doctor couldn't treat my ear. Between the physical pain and the self-inflicted emotional anguish, I couldn't take the torture anymore. I bolted from the doctor's office and found myself wandering the streets and crying, my tears mixing with the rain falling on my face. I looked up at the gray, lowering sky and cried out to God. "Why are you tormenting me? Where is she? When are we going to be together?" I screamed through my weeping.

"Danny?"

I turned, startled, and saw my brother John standing by his idling car. I glanced at my watch and saw that I'd been wandering the streets for over half an hour. He was out looking for me.

"John, I ... I don't know what to do. I can't take it anymore ... Mary ..."

"Come on, Danny," John said. "I know someone who I think can help you."

John took me to see a pastor of a local Baptist church. He counseled with me and gave me a Bible. Once I started reading, it sucked me in as if I were reading parts of my life. Whatever I read about, something similar happened the next day—or I did something and then read about it in the Bible. I felt I was living a very strange life, but it was all for a reason. Something was talking to me. I felt like I was seeing signs in my life, and they gave me hope.

I started going to the Baptist church every Sunday, most of the time by myself. It was my first step back into religion. During the next few months, I read the entire Bible. And it did help me understand more about God and Jesus Christ. But change comes slowly, even when you're doing the right things. Sometimes we're only willing to accept a little bit of light at a time, so that's what God gives us. That's how it was with me.

Through this process, I somehow got the idea into my head that I had to wait three years before I could be with Mary—kind of like the children of Israel having to wander before being allowed into the promised land. I didn't relish the thought of waiting so long, but it did seem like plenty of time to get my life in order. My love for Mary—or at the very least, for the *concept* of her that I'd created in my mind—gave me the will to endure.

And endure I did. After eight months in Arkansas, I moved in with my mom in Richland, Washington. I got a good job at a grocery store (Mary needed a guy who could support her), started paying off debt (Mary deserved a man who didn't owe the bank anything), and got my driver's license back (Mary had a right to be chauffeured—and I hadn't had a license since my DUI conviction). And to make myself the best possible man I could be for Mary, I got a membership at a local gym and started working on a fitness program with a trainer. I wanted to be two hundred pounds of muscle, but my trainer talked me into losing weight first and going from there. She was absolutely right. I dropped about thirty pounds. Not only was I transforming my life, I was transforming my body.

As I improved, I felt compelled to start looking for a church. After attending a couple of different churches, I decided to go back to The Church of Jesus Christ of Latter-day Saints, which I'd grown up in—though I hadn't been back in twenty years. This isn't something I could have done any earlier in my process of transformation. Certain basic habits need to be established before a person is willing to let a church—any church—have the special, unique influence on their lives that only religion can bring. Trying to force it on a person before they're ready is counterproductive and results only in resentment—and greater harm.

Finally, after three and a half years of self-improvement, I felt the time was right to talk to Mary—my purgatory was complete. So I drove down to Santa Cruz to meet with her.

First, though, I spoke with Alan, her boyfriend, who had been my best friend when I'd lived there. As soon as he answered the phone, Alan said, "Danny, it's great to hear from you! It's been so long."

"I know," I said. "Sorry about that. I've been real busy, moving from Arkansas to Washington. I've been working out a lot. And I have been clean and sober for the last three years."

"Wow, that's really something," Alan said. "It's good to hear. So to what do I owe the pleasure?"

"Well, I'm back in town, actually."

"Hey, that's great! Are you moving back down here?"

"No, I'm just visiting," I said. "But I am here for a reason. That's why I wanted to talk to you." I took a deep breath and continued, "We've been friends for how long now, Alan?"

Alan paused. "I dunno. Years."

"Yeah, and it's been great. I really appreciate everything you've done for me—especially helping me out around the time I went to the Farm."

"It wasn't a problem, man."

"So I just wanted to start with that, because what I'm going to tell you is going to be a shocker."

"Lay it on me, man."

I took another deep breath, then blurted out, "I'm in love with Mary."

In the silence I could imagine Alan's mental gears trying to shift without a clutch. After several awkward seconds, he said, "You wanna run that by me again?"

"I am in love with Mary. Like, I can't stop thinking about her."

"You mean, *my girlfriend* Mary?"

"Yeah," I said sheepishly.

"Kay . . ." Alan was struggling for words, so I went on.

"All I came down here to do is tell her how I feel," I said, "and listen to what she has to say in return."

"Um, Danny, I'm not sure—"

"Look, I know this is awkward. I just really, really need to talk with her. And I thought it would be better to talk to you first than to just show up at your door."

"Well, you got *that* right, at least," Alan grumbled.

"So when can I talk to her?"

"Whoa, dude, back up a little. This is . . . weird . . . so how about this: I'll tell her what you told me just now, and then I'll tell you what she says. If she wants to talk with you, then okay, you can talk, but . . . one thing at a time, okay?"

"Yeah, sure, that's fine," I said, truthfully a little disappointed that I wasn't going to be heading over right away. But though I could understand where Alan was coming from—I know I would have been surprised to hear something like that coming from him—at the same time, I was so sure that Mary and I were going to be together that I wasn't worried, in that moment, about not being able to see her soon. "Thanks for doing this for me, Alan. It really means a lot."

"Sure," he said. "I better go and talk to Mary now. She'll be home soon, from picking up our kid from preschool."

"Sounds great," I said.

When he didn't call me that night, I wasn't overly worried. By the third day with no word, I grew concerned. Finally, Alan picked up his phone.

"Hey," he said.

"So how'd it go? What'd she say? When can we meet up?"

"Hold on just a sec," Alan said. "First off, I told her everything you said—how you loved her and everything, just how you said it—and she got a little freaked out. Not gonna lie; you got me a little freaked out too."

"But—but—"

"I mean, you gotta admit, it's kinda weird, coming all the way down here and saying, 'Hey, we've been best buds for years—by the way, I'm in love with your girlfriend.' That's kinda messed up, you know what I mean?"

I couldn't say anything. My mouth was dry.

Alan continued, "So this is the part where you tell me, 'Gotcha! Good joke.' . . . Right, Danny?"

I tried to swallow and found I couldn't, so I said, "No . . . everything I told you was the truth. I'm in love with her. I really, really need to talk with her. Will she see me?"

There was silence for a beat before Alan responded, "Danny, man, I have tried to be nice here, but you're not getting this, so let me put it a different way: you're scaring her, man. We have no clue where you got this idea that you're in love with her, or that in any universe it would somehow be okay to talk to her about it when she's *living with me, her boyfriend*, but this is way, *way* beyond not okay. It's grade A freaky. Mary does not want to meet up with you. She's too scared you'll do something even crazier than this."

My voice caught in my throat as the illusions of the past three years came crashing down around me. This couldn't be happening. My trip down to Santa Cruz was supposed to be the triumphant culmination of a life reformed—not this crushing, devastating obliteration of my soul.

"Well, just, can you put her on the phone for me?" I pleaded. "We don't have to meet in person. I just want to talk."

"Dude, she doesn't even want to talk to you. Look, you come down here, out of the blue, and start saying things that are *terrifying* my girl—who I have a kid with, I'll remind you—like, I don't know what you've been doing since you've been away, but you are *not* okay, man. You're the least okay I've ever seen you, and you know that's saying a heck of a lot."

At this point, I was failing to hold back tears—but at least my sobs weren't audible. I hoped.

"I hope you get your stuff figured out, Danny. I really do."

We hung up.

I collapsed onto the floor.

Mary was terrified of me. The woman I had waited so long for, and changed so much for, wouldn't even speak with me over the phone. Alan's words kept echoing around my skull, and with them a certainty plucked from a song line: *I'm a creep . . . I'm a weirdo.* How could I have been so wrong? How could I have been so blind? So *stupid?* Of *course* they'd react this way! Of *course* there hadn't been some big conspiracy among my friends to bring us together! Now that the illusion was shattered, I recognized the architect of my personal castle of glass: methamphetamines. Only a meth-withdrawing brain—and one severely damaged by years of abuse beforehand—could concoct a plot so outrageous, so out of touch with reality. I cursed my addiction, I cursed myself, and I even cursed God for what I thought I'd felt so surely when reading the Bible. But mostly I felt soul-crushingly disappointed—in myself, for not recognizing the lie before I'd come all the way down to California.

THAT CRUSHING WEIGHT UPON my soul was almost as bad in memory as it was in the first moment I'd felt it. And not only that, but as I lay there in the back of the Grand Cherokee, I felt the sum total of all my mistakes from my entire life piling up on top of me like a mountain. From that first clove cigarette to the final sleeping pill; from Charlie in handcuffs to Hector enraged; from Tracy, pregnant and abandoned, to Sally, married yet estranged—my mind reviewed every mistake I'd ever made. The faces of everyone I'd ever hurt—Oscar, Paul, Kelly, Helen, Alan, and a dozen more—flashed before my eyes. I had wounded each and every one of them through the choices I'd made, the drugs I'd abused, and the lifestyle I'd led. My parents—oh, dear God, my parents—had gone through so much anguish and anxiety because of me, yet every time I'd needed them, my mother or father and my stepparents had welcomed me back into their homes and put up with me until I'd made it literally impossible for them. And of course, the person I'd hurt the most through my rebellious actions had been myself. My body and brain had been permanently injured, my finances were a permanent mess, and my social life was in shambles. In the end, rebellion against what's right is always self-destructive.

The pain in my stomach from twenty-five days without

food was nothing compared to the pain in my soul for my sins. I felt like Alma the Younger:

> Racked with eternal torment, for my soul was harrowed up to the greatest degree and racked with all my sins. Yea, I did remember all my sins and iniquities, for which I was tormented with the pains of hell; yea, I saw that I had rebelled against my God, and that I had not kept his holy commandments. . . . yea, and in fine so great had been my iniquities, that the very thought of coming into the presence of my God did rack my soul with inexpressible horror. (Alma 36:12–14)

And like Alma, I felt this way for *days.* I cried so much I left the blanket beneath me damp, multiple times. Only once in my life had I felt close to this before, and it was the one memory, more than any other, that I did not want to relive. So of course it was the memory I could not escape dwelling on.

WITH THE DISAPPOINTMENT OF Mary's rejection still weighing on me like the weight of a mountainside, I returned home to my mom's house in Richland, Washington. I tried to go back to my rebuilt life—my family, my job—but the loss of my image of Mary and my fantasy dreams of our fictional future together were too much to bear. My mom tried to comfort me, but the wounds were too deep. One night, after work, I sat on a hard chair in the dining room, evaluating my life. Everything I had worked so hard to achieve—my motivation behind every goal, every effort—was a dark abyss of nothingness. My entire self-reinvention had been based on a lie, an illusion. And in my depressed, distraught mind, that meant that I, myself, was a fraud. I felt as empty as my imagined angel Mary had turned out to be.

And if I was a being of emptiness, then the only solution was to embrace the void. Everything else needed to vanish from existence. No, *I* needed to vanish from existence.

My mother left the room to make a call. I went into the kitchen and grabbed a bottle of sleeping pills from the cabinet. I popped one in my mouth and swallowed. Then another. Then another. I kept popping those little capsules until the bottle was empty. I left it on the countertop and went back to the cold, hard dining room chair I'd vacated a moment earlier.

The pills began to kick in very quickly. The slight drip from the kitchen faucet seemed to hang a bit longer each time before falling into the sink. The sounds around me, of the refrigerator and the fluorescent overhead light, sounded as though they were muffled behind a wall of fog. *Good*, I thought. *Let them fade.*

"Danny?" It sounded like my mom was calling me from across the house. Duty reminded me I should answer, but that seemed like too much effort. I turned my heavy head in the direction of the sound and was mildly surprised to find my mother standing right beside me. Part of me wondered when she'd come. "What did you do?" she asked me. Then, more urgently, "Danny, *what did you do?*"

I didn't answer, but she must have seen the empty bottle on the counter in the kitchen, because the next thing I knew, she was calling 911. Then I was in an ambulance. Then an emergency room. I was told later that they decided not to pump my stomach but to let me ride it out. (I guess I hadn't taken enough pills.) I spent that night going in and out of consciousness.

I SPENT MY DAYS in the Grand Cherokee going in and out of consciousness too. I sipped my water and prayed.

AFTER A DAY OR two, I was more coherent, and they brought in a social worker who specialized in attempted suicides.

"Mr. Trotter, why did you try to take your life?"

"Mr. Trotter, do you plan to hurt yourself again?"

"Mr. Trotter, would you consider voluntarily committing yourself to a mental health institution?"

"No," I finally croaked out.

"There's a very reputable psychiatric facility nearby," he said. "I think they could help you."

"They'll just put me on a whole bunch of drugs that my body will completely reject," I told him. "They can't help me there. I won't go."

He frowned, consulted his notes, and then said, "I see. Thank you for your time, Mr. Trotter."

I closed my eyes and tried to rest, grateful he was gone.

The next thing I knew, six police officers stood surrounding my hospital bed, with my mother in the doorway behind them.

"What's going—?" I tried to begin, before one of the cops interrupted me.

"Mr. Trotter, I have a court order here compelling you to a mental health facility, on the recommendation of your social worker."

I cursed that little worm under my breath. Why hadn't he believed me?

"Will you submit to this order?"

"Screw your order!" I shouted, and started to sit up on my bed.

Instant chaos.

The officers immediately grabbed my arms and legs and tried to hold me down, but three years of daily gym workouts had left me pretty strong. Combined with adrenaline, I was unstoppable. I twisted with a roar, and all seven of us toppled onto the floor.

"Grab his hands! Get him cuffed!"

"I've got one—" I pulled my limb away, and the officer swore.

"Ha! Ha, ha, ha!" I laughed.

They tried again, with the same result. A third attempt left us in the same standoff—the best all six of them could do was keep me on the floor; they couldn't cuff me. I was laughing my head off as we wrestled.

Then my mom's voice broke in over the commotion. "Danny, stop it. Please! Please stop fighting!"

If not for her pleading, I would have kept on going until someone had either beaten or drugged me into unconsciousness. But something about my mother's voice made me cease resisting. The cops then handcuffed me and strapped me to a gurney. An ambulance took me to the mental health center, and they rolled me inside an actual padded room, still strapped to the gurney, until I calmed down. And all the while, my mother's desperate pleas reverberated between my ears.

I had attempted to commit suicide. I was almost as far gone from her as it was possible for me to be.

Almost.

———•◆•———

"STOP FIGHTING, DANIEL. COME back to me . . ."

Some of the words were my mother's, but the voice belonged to someone else.

I wiped my eyes and forced my body—slowly, painfully—to sit up. There had been something so undeniably *familiar* about that voice . . .

I looked out the SUV's window and was struck with awe. Hundreds of doves perched on the ground outside, circling my vehicle. They were nowhere else in the campground—not on the trees, not by my fire pit, not even flying in the air—but just around me. They regarded me with placid eyes, softly cooing, as if singing me a lullaby.

In that moment, I was overcome with a tsunami of peace, warmth, and love. God knew me. He understood the trials I had been reliving, and I knew with complete certainty that he had sent these doves to my campsite and my car as a personal message of love to me.

A moment before, I had been in the depths of despair. Now I was encircled about by the arms of God's love as surely and literally as the doves outside were encircling my vehicle. It was both a visual metaphor and a divine sign. I felt again like Alma: "There could be nothing so exquisite and so bitter as were my pains. Yea, and . . . on the other hand, there can be nothing so exquisite and sweet as was my joy" (Alma 36:21).

Tears flowed down my face again—but not tears of regret. This time, they were tears of gratitude that God would show his love for me in such a way. This cleansing I was undertaking was necessary for me. And the physical fast of abstaining from food was only a type and a shadow of the real fast I was undertaking: a cleansing of my spirit from all the sin and wrong I had committed so continuously throughout my life. I learned that day that cleansing leads to healing, and healing leads to the sweet, pure forgiveness that only our loving Heavenly Father can provide.

I also learned for myself that the Sign of the Dove still symbolizes the Holy Ghost, the Comforter sent by God to those who seek and need him—and for good reason. When I saw those doves, I knew I was not alone. I felt the comfort sent to me by God, my Heavenly Father. I knew that I would be okay.

And that I was very, very close to achieving God's goals for my fast.

SEEING THE DOVES GAVE me a renewed sense of strength. I was still physically weaker than I'd ever been before, but I felt a new, different type of strength emerging underneath my weakness—a strength of will and spirit, of faith and character. With that energy, and once the doves had flown away, I drove to the small gas station and convenience store near the entrance of Riverside State Park. I'd been running the SUV's heater at night to stay warm, which meant I was low on fuel. I filled the gas tank and put air in the tires. Then I went inside the store and bought a sports drink.

My body needed the electrolytes, but drinking the beverage wasn't an option. I went out to the parking lot and poured the whole bottle out on the ground. Then I drove back to my campsite, empty bottle in hand.

After more than three weeks without food, my body was nearing the end of its rope, and I could feel the strength draining out of me. Basic hygiene felt like running a marathon. My toothbrush was as difficult to lift as a thirty-pound dumbbell. I'd long ago stopped walking to the park restrooms with the showers and started driving there instead. Now, even that became too much. They were a hundred yards away.

Who's going to smell me anyway? I asked myself.

After that decision, my biggest task each day was climbing out of the SUV to void my bladder on the ground. It took all my strength to do just that one simple task.

When my next trip outside looked insurmountable, I started filling up that empty bottle.

Several times, anxiety overwhelmed me. I'm sure it was exacerbated by the lack of food. It felt as though a million fiery ants were crawling up and down my skin. I had to clench my hands to fight the urge to scratch. Peeling off my outer layer and crawling out seemed preferable. But I endured. I sat in my discomfort and drank in the experience. I faced it and felt it like I'd never faced or felt anything before. I learned from this experience that it's better to face our trials head-on than to search for a distraction that takes our minds away from them. We can let fear push us around like a bully—I'd lived much of my life that way. But I would no longer run away.

Run away. Seek distractions. Those thoughts reminded me of another time from my past—this one more recent than most of the memories I'd been reliving. But the seeds that grew into this mistake took a long, long time to grow.

MY FIRST JOB AFTER high school was as a porter in a local grocery store. One day, as I was lifting some heavy tubs of ice, I felt something pop in my back. I didn't know it then, but it would never be the same. My uncle, who was a chiropractor, tried to help me, but over time, my problems got worse. By the time I was living in Arkansas with John, I needed major surgery (which would turn out to be the first of four). It was recovering from this first operation that led me to the gym rat's life in Washington. By 2009, I was busy working as a trainer—and not just for anyone. This was a fourteen-year-old kid who had NHL-league talent.

"Come on," I said to him. "It's your turn on the leg press machine."

"You got it, coach," he said.

He completed his first set, and I could tell he'd improved since the week before. "How'd that feel?" I asked.

"Not bad," he said. "Can you put another plate on?"

"You bet." I chuckled and added, "You keep this up, you'll have bigger legs than me." I grabbed a hundred-pound plate from the weight rack and rotated my torso back toward the machine.

Pop.

I gritted my teeth to keep from swearing.

"You okay, Coach?"

I shoved the plate on the machine and secured it, unable to hide my grimace.

"Just fine," I managed to grind out. "Do your set."

As he did, I tried to massage my sciatic nerve. Pain shot down my leg like liquid fire. *Oh no,* I thought. *Not again.*

At first I tried to work through my pain while getting physical therapy, but eventually I applied for workers' compensation, since it was an on-the-job injury. My relationship with my manager was already strained because there was a training director position available that I thought I deserved, but he'd given it to someone else. This just made it worse. On top of that, I'd been dating a coworker named Karrie and had grown close to her young son. And right about that time, she chose to dump me.

It was a perfect storm of every type of pain and stress you can imagine. It looked so much easier to just give in to despair than to keep enduring.

One weekend night, my back was giving me tremendous pain, and I was desperate to find relief. I couldn't locate a massage therapist, so I went to a place that called itself a "massage center"—but that was a thinly veiled euphemism. In fairness, they did give me a massage. But then the woman offered more—much, much more—for a little extra fee.

Karrie had just broken my heart—another perfect-looking relationship coming to a failed end. I hadn't been with a woman, at that point, in four and a half years. It wasn't fair, I told myself.

Maybe it wasn't, but that in no way excused what I did next. I gave in to her temptation. For the first and only time, I paid for sex.

I tried not to care about what I had done, but I couldn't. I felt dirty. I knew I had participated in further ruining that woman's life. I hadn't put her in that situation, nor could I get her out of it, but I had contributed to it continuing, and that was guilt enough. It was a burden around my life as heavy as Jacob Marley's chains, and just as ponderous. I carried the burden with me for the next two days, until finally I felt I would explode if I did not confide to *someone*.

So I called my dad up on the phone. "I have to tell you something, Dad. Okay?"

"I'm listening, son."

"I—oh, I feel so awful just *thinking* about it—two days ago, I . . . I paid for sex. I slept with a prostitute, Dad. And I've felt miserable about it ever since."

And then my dad did something I did not expect. He said quietly, "Tell me what happened."

So I did. And by the end, the chain felt lighter round my neck.

"Was that the only time?" he asked.

"Yes," I said. "I'm never doing that again. I never want to feel this way."

"I love you, son."

My throat choked up.

"Thank you for telling me this. For trusting me. I want you to know that you are still my son, and no matter what mistakes you make, I'll always love you. And there is hope for you."

"There is?"

"There is. You can be forgiven for this mistake—and not just by me, by God. Remember that old scripture I used to read you, about how you know if a man's repented of his sins?"

That sounded familiar, but I admitted I couldn't recall it specifically.

"A man's repented if he confesses and forsakes his sins," Dad said. "And that's when God forgives him. You've confessed to me just now, and it sounds to me like you forsook this sin right away. That sounds like real repentance to me, son."

I started crying.

"That's not all you need to do," he continued. "You need to pray for forgiveness from God, and you need to make it up to this woman, if you can—though that might not be possible."

"I'll try," I replied.

"I'm glad that you've called to tell me this."

I wasn't able to find the woman I'd slept with, but I did ask God for his forgiveness. And slowly, over time, my guilt was swept away.

I learned from that experience that before we can find forgiveness from God, sometimes we need to seek forgiveness from our fellow man. My earthly father offered it to me with love, and I will be forever grateful to him for that gift.

MAYBE THAT WAS WHAT I needed now. *Come back to me*, something whispered in my mind. I pulled out my phone, and with trembling thumb, dialed up my dad. He answered on the second ring.

"Dan!" he answered. "How's your camping trip?"

I remembered then I hadn't told him I'd be fasting. "It's . . . it's going great," I answered, somewhat honestly.

"What have you been up to?" he asked, concern tinging his voice.

"Dad, I—I want to come back to church."

There was nothing but silence on the other end. Whatever he'd been expecting, I knew this had not been it. But just like with our call two years before, he was as supportive and helpful as any son could ask a father to be.

I came out to the wilderness to get closer to my Heavenly Father, but in doing so, I grew closer to my earthly father as well.

That night, I had another dream—but this one was much different than the ones that came before. For the first time, I felt the adversary's absence and knew that he would not appear.

I saw a road that led straight up into the sky. And I saw the people traveling along it. They looked like they were human, but something about them seemed to show that they were from planets other than Earth. They embarked on UFO-like ships, and one by one, each silver disc ascended into heaven.

I wanted nothing more than to join them. Heaven was my goal, and here it was, right in front of me! I started to move forward, toward the ships. Then something stopped me, like a firm but gentle hand on my shoulder. And someone whispered in my ear, "Now is not your time, Daniel. There is still much work for you to do."

"But I want to go with them more than anything!"

"Your body is close to letting you go," the voice admitted, "but now is not your time. You must stay and do the work that only you can do."

I looked down, crestfallen. I had so wanted to ascend with them!

"Don't be discouraged, Daniel," the voice said kindly. "If you stay true and do your work, then you will be transported up to heaven, too—exalted on high. According to your faithfulness, it can be done—even for you."

I looked back up. The departing silver ships now twinkled like distant stars. "What is the work that I must do?"

"Come back," said the voice. "Come back to me, and I will let you know."

DAY THIRTY OF MY fast dawned cold and bright. But I was fading quickly. The lethargy had reached a new oppressiveness. My bottle was almost full, but I lacked the strength to leave the car's back seat. So I did the only thing I could: I prayed.

All day.

"Help me," I pleaded. "Give me the strength to keep going."

I reviewed with my Heavenly Father everything I'd done while at the park—the memories I'd relived, the dreams I'd dreamed, the communication that I'd had with Sally and my earthly father. I pondered on how much I'd changed over the years, and over these last thirty days. I'd felt the goodness, love, and mercy of God, as well as the temptations of evil like I'd never felt them before. But scariest of all was clearly seeing myself, the natural man—and the consequences of following those natural appetites without restriction, both for myself and others. My body and my mind had been torn to shreds by drugs, and even my healthier lifestyle now would never fully repair the damage. I'd taken Tracy—and others—down with me into my addictions, and now their lives were forever worse for what I'd done. And Mary—I'd hurt her deeply while telling myself I loved her. Things like these I couldn't make right on my own. So I would have to trust in God to sort it out one day.

One thing was certain: I never wanted to hurt anyone like that ever again. And I realized my heart had changed.

About eight thirty that night, with tears running down my face, I asked, "God, are we done yet? Can I go home now—please?" I pleaded and begged, then let my little Bible fall open. On the page it opened to, my eyes focused on two words: *go home*.

My prayer was answered. I had done all that I needed to do—I had gone through the repentance process and had a true change of heart. I had committed to my father to come back to church, and I was going to live up to that commitment. And now I was finally being released from my fast.

The burden of my lethargy lifted instantly. Adrenaline, excitement, and sheer joy coursed through my veins instead. "Hallelujah!" I exclaimed. Suddenly able to move, I packed up the Grand Cherokee, all the while praising and thanking God. I kept on yelling "Hallelujah!" as I packed, and I shouted it at the top of my lungs as I drove home. Home! I was finally going home!

My house was only about ten minutes away from the campsite. Before I knew it, I was back home.

Sally wasn't there. She'd gone on a work retreat and wouldn't be back for two more days.

Alone, I started juicing fruits and vegetables. I didn't

want to rush my eating, but I couldn't help it. I was so hungry. Shortly, my body went into shock, and I threw up all I had eaten. I ate again and then threw it all back up. Finally, I kept something down.

My body recovered, and two days later, I was out getting snow tires on the Chrysler 300. I dropped the car off and decided to take a walk around the strip mall parking lot. And even though it was the same strip mall it had been when I'd left, it looked different. The little shops, instead of looking like drab outlets of commercialism, brought back pleasant memories. The people walking around were no longer just shapes in my path—they were brothers and sisters. The whole world looked different. And I wondered, *Did this place change, or did I?*

I went into a Michaels store and wandered around. The pieces of prefabricated art no longer seemed like commercial reproductions. Instead, I saw the artistry of the original piece and recognized the talents that went into creating each one. One of my brothers or sisters had shared their gifts with me, and with many other people. No, I decided, the world had not changed. I had.

I walked back to the auto shop as if I were walking on air, filled with peace, joy, happiness, and calm.

My fast had finally ended on Saturday, November 12, 2011, well after nine p.m.

And two days later, I realized that I was utterly trans-formed.

EPILOGUE

AFTER MY FAST, I thought that Heavenly Father was going to fix everything in my life. And he did. But since his ways are not our ways, he didn't fix things in the way that I expected.

My going back to church drove a wedge between me and Sally, and when faced with the prospect of another back surgery for me, our marriage ended. I really couldn't blame her; my last one had knocked me off my feet for an entire year. I moved in with my dad. Everything I owned fit underneath the bed in his guest room. But stuff didn't matter to me anymore.

It might seem odd that life got harder for me after my fast, not easier. But that's the way life works. When we want to do the most good, we're faced with the greatest opposition. The test is what we decide to do in those times. Because of my newfound conversion, I was finally able to stay faithful through the trial. My fast had left me physically weaker than I had ever been before, but I returned from that wilderness a different kind of strong. Through my willingness to sacrifice everything—even my own life, had it been necessary—I had gained a spiritual strength that I'm determined to maintain for the rest of my life, and forever.

Each week, life got a little better as my focus turned to

service. I became the missionary taxi. I visited church members and did home teaching. I went to all church functions. I would even go to the temple with my dad once a week and meditate in the waiting room while he did an endowment session. (Just because you don't have a temple recommend doesn't mean you can't go to the temple and feel the Spirit!)

I scheduled weekly meetings with my bishop, who suggested that I retake the missionary lessons. It was a brilliant idea. Starting from scratch, I learned line upon line, precept upon precept, and I began to understand the scriptures like never before.

And through it all, I *chose* to be happy, no matter my circumstances. God had made me strong enough to do it. Keeping the commandments kept me safe from depression, regret, sorrow, and shame.

I dated a little bit in Spokane, but nothing worked out. The interest was always one sided. Either I really liked a woman and she didn't like me, or it was the other way around—the frustratingly familiar story of my entire romantic life.

While watching BYUtv one day, I felt prompted to move to Salt Lake. I didn't know anyone there besides a couple of cousins—my family was mostly in California and Washington State—but I knew it was something I had to do. So I did it. I'd spent my life doing what I wanted to do, but now I was going to do what the Lord wanted me to do. I left on Halloween, 2013.

I'm eternally grateful that I did. Through a series of circumstances that to others might seem mundane but to me were miraculous, I met my wife, Julianne. The only problem was that she was a missionary at the time (although she was about my age). But if I could wait for thirty days to eat, then I could wait the nine months it would take for her to finish her mission. And I did. This time, thankfully, the Lord, the woman, and I were all on the same wavelength. My Heavenly Parents picked my bride, and we couldn't be happier together. Julianne is, in real life, all the things I once imagined Mary to be—all those things and much, much more.

Six weeks after Julianne finished her mission, we were sealed together in the Los Angeles Temple. It was a white wedding—everyone dressed in white clothing, even the guests—something that happens only with special permission from the temple matron. The Spirit was so strong that almost everyone was weeping. I was no exception. We shared our first kiss over that altar, which had once belonged to the Salt Lake Temple, my favorite.

It was perfect.

Life since then has been life. Despite everything I've been through, I'm still not a perfect person. And as much as I adore Julianne, occasionally, neither is she—though she's much, much closer to it than I am! And adversities still come, no matter how righteous we may be. Trials keep us humble. They refine us. They make us that different kind of strong that we must be to return to live with our Heavenly Parents. These mortal experiences teach us how to become like them, if we are willing to learn. Even the worst of them—like the ones I've been through—truly can be for our good. If we choose to allow God to guide our lives, He will make all adversity transform us into luminous beings like He is. He'll make us strong—just not the kind of strong that we usually suppose.

A different kind of strong.

───────•◆•───────

Made in the USA
Las Vegas, NV
22 August 2021

28675142R00085